Seven
Spiritual Gifts
of Waiting

Seven
Spiritual Gifts
of Waiting

Patience

Loss of Control

Living in the Present

Compassion

Gratitude

Humility

Trust in God

HOLLY W. WHITCOMB

Augsburg Books
MINNEAPOLIS

SEVEN SPIRITUAL GIFTS OF WAITING

Large-quantity purchases or custom editions of this book are available at a discount
from the publisher. For more information, contact the sales department at Augsburg
Fortress, Publishers, 1-800-328-4648, or write to: Sales Director, Augsburg Fortress,
Publishers, P. O. Box 1209, Minneapolis, MN 55440-1209.

Scripture passages are from the *New Revised Standard Version* of the Bible, copyright ©
1946, 1952, 1971, 1989 by the Division of Christian Education of the National Council
of the Churches of Christ in the USA. Used by permission.

Library of Congress Cataloging-in-Publication Data
Whitcomb, Holly W. (Holly Wilson), 1953-
    Seven spiritual gifts of waiting / by Holly W. Whitcomb.
        p. cm.
    Includes bibliographical references (p.   ).
    ISBN 0-8066-5128-8 (pbk. : alk. paper)
    1. Expectation (Psychology)—Religious aspects—Christianity. 2. Trust
in God. 3. Patience—Religious aspects—Christianity. 4. Christian life.
I. Title.
BV4647.E93W45 2005
248.4—dc22   2005024212

Cover design by Diana Running; cover photo copyright © Donovan Reese/Getty
Images. Used by permission.
Book design by Michelle L. N. Cook

For additional acknowledgment information, see page 126.

The paper used in this publication meets the minimum requirements of American
National Standard for Information Sciences—Permanence of Paper for Printed Library
Materials, ANSI Z329.48-1984. ♾ ™

Manufactured in the U.S.A.

To the people of Redeemer United Church of Christ,

Sussex, Wisconsin,

and to Pastor Bob Ullman,

all courageous people-in-waiting . . .

after the fire

WAITING IS THE INGREDIENT

NECESSARY TO A LIFE OF QUALITY.

—*Gertrud Mueller Nelson*

Contents

Introduction

I hate waiting just about as much as anything in this world. I will not eat at a restaurant if I have to stand and wait. I will not even *approach* a freeway entrance if there is any possibility I will have to sit in traffic. In Milwaukee, I will drive twenty extra minutes, the complete length of State Street or Wisconsin Avenue, in order to avoid coming to a standstill on the freeway. If I have to wait in line at the grocery store, I will bossily charge up to the manager and ask why customers are waiting and suggest they open a new checkout lane without delay.

I obviously could use a good dose of Advent.

The season of Advent, more than any other time of the church year, invites us to embrace the spiritual discipline of waiting. The season of Advent will not be rushed. The Advent carols must be sung, the Advent candles must be lighted week by week, and the doors of the Advent Calendar must be opened day by day. Christmas will finally come when all the expectant Scriptures have been read and when the baby has finally been born.

Twenty-two years ago I stood at the pulpit of Redeemer Church on the first Sunday of Advent, waiting. I was twenty-nine years old and nine-months pregnant with our second child. Looking like a Mack truck that Sunday, I preached about Advent while I waited to give birth. Being pregnant during Advent is a rich and marvelous experience. Pregnancy, perhaps more than anything else, teaches the gifts of waiting. That year I was waiting not only for a baby to be born, but for other things as well. I was waiting to be employed and was looking for a church. I was waiting to make friends. I was waiting for a time to stop grieving the small university community we had just left. I was waiting for money to buy a new furnace. I was waiting for Milwaukee to feel like home.

Every stage of our lives involves some new form of waiting. When our children are tiny, we wait years for a good night's sleep. When our children are toddlers, we wait eagerly for the time when they will no longer wear diapers, can take a bath on their own, and get dressed by themselves. When our children are teenagers and driving, we often wait anxiously until we hear the front door close and know they are safely home. And at any stage of life, we can experience waiting for the results of medical tests. This kind of waiting is perhaps the hardest of all. A weekend can seem like an eternity if we are waiting to find out whether a tumor is malignant or benign.

Waiting presents an enormous challenge. We are impatient, I-can-fix-it kinds of people . . . but not all situations can be fixed. We assume that everything in life can be made better by taking action, but sometimes it just isn't so.

A writer whose retreat I was attending talked about a single friend who, at age forty, decided she would like to adopt a child. This woman did her homework and talked to several adoption agencies. When she was told that the process of adopting a child would take at the very least a year, she said, "Forget it. I just don't have that kind of time."[1]

We shrink when we are presented with situations where action does no good at all. We deplore the passivity of waiting. Yet waiting is an enormous opportunity if we regard it as a wise teacher. Waiting offers us a great deal when we choose to learn. Hear these words from thirteenth-century Persian poet Rumi:

> This being human is a guest
> house. Every morning
> a new arrival.
>
> A joy, a depression, a meanness,
> some momentary awareness comes
> as an unexpected visitor.

Welcome and attend them all!
Even if they're a crowd of sorrows,
who violently sweep your house
empty of its furniture, still,
treat each guest honorably.
He may be clearing you out
for some new delight.

The dark thought, the shame, the malice,
meet them at the door laughing,
and invite them in.

Be grateful for whoever comes,
because each has been sent
as a guide from beyond.[2]

Waiting is an important guest to honor in the guest house of our humanity. If we consciously allow waiting to be our teacher, we can accommodate waiting more peacefully. If we welcome waiting as a spiritual discipline, waiting will present its spiritual gifts. Waiting contains some of our richest spiritual opportunities if we are conscious enough and courageous enough to name them and live into them.

Bingo halls and casinos often post the sign, "You must be present to win." In order to convert the inescapable lessons of waiting into deliberate spiritual gifts, we, too, have to be present; we need to pay attention. We need to actively participate in this dramatic conversion from waiting as something to be endured to waiting as a gift.

The Bible has many dramatic stories about waiting. The Israelites wandered in the wilderness for forty years waiting to get into the Promised Land. Jacob waited fourteen years before winning the hand of Rachel, his beloved. The Apostle Paul waited over and over to be released from prison. Jesus waited forty days in the desert tempted by the devil.

In her beloved hymn "Lead On, O Cloud of Yahweh," hymn writer Ruth Duck affirms:

> We are not lost, though wandering,
>   for by your light we come,
> and we are still God's people.
>   The journey is our home.[3]

"The journey is our home." And our journey will always include waiting. If we are going to continue to live, we are going to continue to wait. The good news is that the discipline of waiting offers us seven spiritual gifts:

The first gift of waiting is patience.

The second gift of waiting is loss of control.

The third gift of waiting is the living in the present.

The fourth gift of waiting is compassion.

The fifth gift of waiting is gratitude.

The sixth gift of waiting is humility.

The seventh gift of waiting is trust in God.

May the God who loves us help us all learn how to wait.

The First Gift of Waiting: Patience

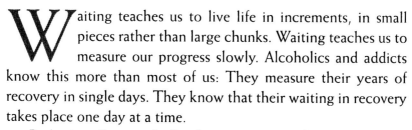

Waiting teaches us to live life in increments, in small pieces rather than large chunks. Waiting teaches us to measure our progress slowly. Alcoholics and addicts know this more than most of us: They measure their years of recovery in single days. They know that their waiting in recovery takes place one day at a time.

Psalm 25 talks specifically about waiting on God: "You are the God of my salvation; for you I wait all day long" (25:5). It is hard to wait on God. Whether we're freeing ourselves from addiction, healing from a long illness, adopting a baby, or waiting for word to come through about a job or a house or a school, it is hard to trust the slow unfolding of God's action. God's time is different from our time. In God's time, we are often waiting for the bigger picture but must be content with each small piece. When we are waiting, we put one foot in front of the other every morning and every evening. Waiting teaches us patience.

> *Do you have the patience to wait*
> *till your mud settles and the water is clear?*
> *Can you remain unmoving*
> *Till the right action arises by itself?*[1]
> —Lao-tzu, *Tao Te Ching*

PATIENCE MEANS TRUSTING THERE'S NO QUICK FIX.

Many chapters of our lives require long commitments. Whole chapters of our lives require waiting that goes on for years. But this kind of waiting is counter-cultural. Our modern society would have us believe that there is a "quick fix" for everything, if we hire the right specialist or consume the right product. It just isn't so.

Every time I begin writing a book, I prop up on my desk a greeting card that pictures a long, stone path with these words: "The journey of a thousand miles begins with a single step." This reminds me there is no quick fix and that I am simply going to have to show up at the empty page time after time.

Last night I talked to my son who told me that he had studied three-hundred hours for one of his national financial exams. Someone might spend years working on a Ph.D., taking classes, writing a dissertation, going through oral and written exams. It frequently takes four to ten years and often requires a huge balancing act between family, paid work, and study.

For someone taking care of an elderly relative who is ailing, it's also a huge project in patience. It may require hiring a home-health aide, or helping a loved one move into a retirement community or investigate assisted living. It may mean working part-time instead of full-time in order to take on the caretaking. It may mean daily visits, counting out pills, washing clothes and bedding, or cooking food. It may mean daily or weekly visits to a rehabilitation center or a physician's office. In many families the care of an ailing and elderly relative takes months or decades. These kinds of scenarios require a long-term perspective and years of patience.

Rachel Naomi Remen, M.D., a doctor and counselor to the chronically ill and dying, has had Crohn's disease for over fifty years. In 1981, however, she began experiencing frightening new symptoms she could not explain: uncontrollable shaking, a fever of 106 degrees in the midst of normal activities, and extreme, debilitating fatigue. Like the woman in the Bible with the hemorrhage, Dr. Remen continually sought assistance from doctors, but she became discouraged when no one could help and no one would listen. As her symptoms became more frequent and more severe, as she became more and more fearful, she decided to seek help one more time from a doctor with whom she sat on an advisory board. Because he was part of an HMO, she knew he was not allowed to visit with her for more than fifteen minutes, and she was skeptical about how much clarity and support fifteen minutes could provide.

Dr. Remen writes,

> There was a soft knock on the door and Dr. Smith entered. He greeted me and then spent a few minutes sitting quietly and reading over the lab results and X-ray studies I had brought with me. Then he leaned toward me and said, "Tell me why you have come."
>
> I looked into his face and saw a genuine concern. I began to tell him all the things I was experiencing, starting with the more commonplace and finally including such things as the strange taste that often awakened me from sleep, and the times when I suddenly lost all sense of direction and was unable to remember how to get home. My voice shook a little. He continued to listen.
>
> Slowly I began to tell him other things, things I had not told anyone else. . . . Eventually I said it all and then I just cried. . . .
>
> Dr. Smith said nothing to interrupt and just listened closely. When I had finished, he asked a few questions that showed me that he had heard and fully understood. Then he reached for my hand and told me he realized how hard things were. He validated my concerns. . . . He assured me that eventually whatever this was would declare itself more clearly and when it did, if there was a surgical solution, he would be there. He looked at me and smiled. "We will wait together," he told me.[2]

Several months later when an X-ray revealed that Rachel Remen had a huge abscess hidden deep in her abdomen, it was Dr. Smith who did her surgery. Rachel Remen came to trust Dr.

Smith because he did not pretend that her medical condition was simple to figure out. He did not bluster ahead with a quick fix, but waited patiently until the true cause of her symptoms came to light.

When we have to wait without knowing the answers, without knowing what's ahead, we are nudged into a new perspective. Waiting without immediate solutions presents us with an opportunity to lean into the unknowing, to let go of the false promise of a quick fix, and to grow in patience. When we can embrace the gift of patience that waiting offers, we can trust beyond the moment.

PATIENCE INVITES US TO TRUST THE FULLNESS OF GOD'S TIME.

> Have you not known? Have you not heard?
> The LORD is the everlasting God,
> the Creator of the ends of the earth.
> [God] does not faint or grow weary;
> [God's] understanding is unsearchable.
> [God] gives power to the faint,
> and strengthens the powerless.
> Even youths will faint and be weary,
> and the young will fall exhausted;
> but those who wait for the LORD
> shall renew their strength,
> they shall mount up with wings like eagles,
> they shall run and not be weary,
> they shall walk and not faint.
> —Isaiah 40:28-31

It is very hard to wait. We want to take our lives into our own hands and make things happen right away. Yet the Bible continually asks us to trust the fullness of God's time.

But when *the fullness of time* had come, God sent his Son.
—Galatians 4:4a

With all wisdom and insight God has made known to us the mystery of God's will, according to God's good pleasure set forth in Christ, as a plan for *the fullness of time*, to gather up all things in Christ, things in heaven and things on earth.
—Ephesians 1:8b-10[3]

Now after John was arrested, Jesus came to Galilee, proclaiming the good news of God, and saying, *"The time is fulfilled,* and the kingdom of God has come near; repent, and believe in the good news."
—Mark 1:14-15

Jesuit Pierre Teilhard de Chardin says:

Above all, trust in the slow work of God. We are, quite naturally, impatient in everything to reach the end without delay.

We should like to skip the intermediate stages; we are impatient of being on the way to something unknown, something new. And yet, it is the law of all progress that it is made by passing through some stages of instability . . . and that it may take a very long time.[4]

There is a rightness about God's time: a ripeness, a maturation, a waiting that is worth it. It is as if some of the geographic, physical, emotional, and spiritual pieces have to gestate before coming together. So often, *in retrospect,* we can look back at something and say, "Oh, yes. I wouldn't have been ready before. It makes sense why I had to wait and why this is happening now."

Most of us hate the word "no." "No" is almost obscene in this culture of immediate gratification and overconsumption, but sometimes we have to endure it anyway. When we hear that word, our hearts sink, and we genuinely wonder, at least for a few minutes, how we will carry on. Yet every one of us can look back at those times when someone refused us and somehow we survived. We may not only have survived, but also grown better, stronger, perhaps even happier as a result of that initial rejection. It is possible that being denied fosters growth. Regrettably, this sounds very Puritanical and long-suffering, but I think it is true. As I was thinking about the "nos" in our lives, I thought of something Madeleine L'Engle wrote about rejection:

> Experience is painfully teaching me that what seems a NO . . . is often the essential prelude to a far greater YES. . . . During the two years when *A Wrinkle in Time* was consistently being rejected by publisher after publisher, I often went out alone at night . . . and shouted at God; "Why don't you let it get accepted? Why are you letting me have all these rejection slips? You know it's a good book! I wrote it for you! So why doesn't anybody see it?"
>
> But when *Wrinkle* was finally published, it was exactly the right moment for it, and if it had been published two years earlier it might well have dropped into a black pit of oblivion.[5]

I remember a time when my hopes were crushed with a "no." It was March of 1978. I was plugging away in New Haven finishing up my last year of seminary, knowing I would be moving out to Iowa City, Iowa, to join my husband, John, who was doing his internship in internal medicine. I didn't have a job yet, and the months were rolling along. After weeks of conversation with United Church of Christ executives in Des Moines and significant dollars' worth of long-distance phone bills, I finally got an interview with the search committee of Olds United Church of Christ in Olds, Iowa. After the interview that evening, my rational mind told me that this church was not the place for me: It was a fifty-mile commute; the town of two-hundred people was way out in the boondocks; it was a church of elderly hog farmers; and deep down I knew full well that a suburban girl like me was not going to thrive communing with the livestock. Yet my heart was absolutely set on it. It was simply all there was.

With genuine eagerness, I told the search committee I was willing to come if they would have me. Finally, a phone call came. They said "no." They didn't want me. I was inconsolable. For weeks and weeks after that, I was sure no good could possibly come from that rejection. The "no" of that rejection left me baffled and depressed. Only in retrospect was I able to understand that, had the placement worked out, it would have been a disaster. God had been preparing me all along to accept a ministry for which I was much more suited. Five months later, a call came to be the pastor of Faith United Church of Christ in Iowa City. This was a marvelous little congregation that stretched me and affirmed me. It was in the university town of Iowa City where we lived and was even within walking distance of the house my husband and I had bought. Certainly the first "no" had been a prelude to a far greater "yes."

Over and over in our lives we are bewildered and disappointed about timing. We may despair. We may think God has forgotten us or is actively defeating our well-laid plans. We may believe God is not answering our prayers, or that the answer is always "no." Frequently, it is in the fullness of God's time that we have the opportunity to grow and bloom.

In difficult times of waiting, I have always appreciated psychologist Jack Kornfield's clarifying questions:

How have I treated this difficulty thus far?
What does this problem ask me to let go of?
What great lesson might it be able to teach me?
What is the gold, the value, hidden in this situation?[6]

Whenever I ask myself these questions, something shakes loose. I can usually find considerable substance in my answers about the power of my ego, or about God's timing, or about something I am holding onto tightly that I need to release.

If you find yourself in a place of waiting, you might want to spend a little time with these questions and see if something becomes clearer for you. Try stepping back to look at the bigger picture, take in the perspective of your whole life, and acknowledge that this time of waiting is only one chapter. Let this lesson of waiting sink in: Patience is a standing invitation to trust in God's timing.

PATIENCE OPENS US TO ACTIVE WAITING.

"Don't let the time do you. You do the time."

My hairdresser quoted these words to me recently as I was getting my hair cut. She has been waiting years for her son to be released from prison on an armed-robbery charge, and the waiting is hard. She attends a support group for family members whose loved ones are serving time. The group is led by an ex-con who says, "This is how we survive on the inside and how all of you can survive on the outside: Don't let the time do you. You do the time." This kind of active waiting is good advice for anyone who waits.

Henri Nouwen and his colleagues write,

[T]rue patience is the opposite of a passive waiting in which we let things happen and allow others to make the decisions. Patience means to enter actively into the thick of life and to fully bear the suffering within and around us. Patience is the capacity to see, hear, touch, taste, and smell as fully as possible the inner and outer events of our lives. It is to enter our lives with open eyes, ears, and hands so that we really know what is happening. Patience is an extremely difficult discipline precisely because it counteracts our unreflective impulse to flee or to fight. . . .

Patience requires us to go beyond the choice between fleeing or fighting. . . . It calls for discipline because it goes against the grain of our impulses. Patience involves staying with it, living it through, listening carefully to what presents in the here and now. Patience means stopping on the road when someone in pain needs immediate attention. Patience means overcoming the fear of a controversial subject. It means paying attention to shameful memories and searching for forgiveness without having to forget. It means welcoming sincere criticism and evaluating changing conditions. In short, patience is a willingness to be influenced even when this requires giving up control and entering into unknown territory.[7]

Think of people you have known or have read about who actively waited. People healing from surgery follow doctors' orders for medications, physical therapy, diet, and exercise to restore their long-term wellness. Those who suffer violence and trauma may devote years of therapy to regain their wholeness. People who want to change unfair systems battle injustice and work faithfully for civil rights even though they may not see change in their lifetimes.

Three years ago my mother discovered that she had colon cancer and was diagnosed at stage four. Most of us, upon hearing this bad news, would have closed up shop and wallowed in anxiety and depression. My mother moved into active waiting, hoping for a few more years of quality life, and she is amazingly proactive in caring for herself. She intentionally chooses to live positively and to nurture a healthy lifestyle. She has eliminated trans fats from her diet; each day she prepares brightly colored food, including seven to eight servings of fruits and vegetables; and at age eighty-four, she still walks six miles a day. She is trying to banish worry from her life and determinedly cultivates friendship because she knows that the absence of worry and the comfort of friends have healing power. She is strengthened every week by her active waiting. Active waiting empowers her, makes her happier, and instills hope for her future.

Too often we think of patience as equivalent to long-suffering, as some kind of passive acceptance. Patience is actually demanding, assertive, and complex. It calls for looking at the bigger picture and assessing timing and trade-offs. It requires a keen emotional intelligence that considers what is at stake. When is it time to act? What steps are appropriate? What actions will help us *participate* in the waiting?

When we face an extended period of waiting, we have an opportunity to engage in a radical kind of patience that can take us beyond surviving, to thriving. We can partner with the waiting rather than treat it as the enemy. We can involve ourselves in an active waiting that opens doors, creates opportunities, and stretches our minds, bodies, and souls. While waiting may necessitate a certain powerlessness, this does not mean giving up intelligence, action, and hope. Active waiting teaches us to trust that each small step is part of a larger process—a process in which we can participate with steady determination and lively expectation.

PATIENCE GIVES US TIME TO BE AVAILABLE TO OTHERS.

Waiting presents us with a choice: to fret in isolation or to shift into an expansive patience that includes those around us. The gift in this kind of patient waiting is realizing that we have the time to be available to others. Often when we are waiting for something, we are not waiting alone. The setting may be something as common as waiting in an airport for a delayed plane, or as complex as waiting in a hospital lounge for news about the results of a loved one's surgery. Whether we are empathizing with the mother whose delayed plane is causing her to miss her daughter's birthday party, or sympathizing with the husband who is waiting for the surgeon's report on his wife's condition, we have the opportunity to really be *with* each other, in the fullest sense of the word.

Recently, as I was working in my office, I looked up at a picture above my desk of my dad giving me a hug. It is one of the last pictures I have of him before he died. One of my father's best gifts was availability. When you talked to him, he made you feel as if you were the most important person on earth. He offered his full attention. He never read a magazine or talked on the phone or looked bored while he was spending time with you. He always sat quietly in rapt attention, waiting eagerly to hear your story unfold. That's why children loved him. If a small child talked to him while crawling on the floor, my dad would engage that child and get down and crawl on the floor, too. If you started a conversation with him while you were up on a ladder painting your house, he would grab a ladder and a can of paint and continue the conversation up there. Corporate trainers and neurolinguistic experts would have had nothing new to teach my dad about cultivating empathy. He knew it inherently. He was somehow born knowing how to be available: willing to stop, get on your level, and listen patiently with full attention.

Whether we like it or not, children and old people cultivate in us the practice of being available. When we're with little children, they demand our attention and know immediately when we're drifting off or becoming distracted. They ask that we get down on their level and enter their world. That may mean pretending the pine needles on your lap are a dish of spaghetti or running around the backyard on a broomstick pretending it's a horse. Being with young children is often healing because they require our undivided attention. This means we can't get distracted with worry or anxiety about our own adult lives. We get to take a vacation from all that when we are with them, being wholly present and focused in the moment.

It is the same thing with some older people. They often require our patience as we enter their world. It may take five minutes for them to get to the door. It may take ten rings for them to pick up the phone. They may have trouble hearing and trouble walking. We learn to move more slowly around old people, to understand that crossing the street takes time and possibly assistance. Conversation often requires patience, too, as their talk may be filled with repetitions as well as detours into long stories and anecdotes. We may find ourselves hearing recitations of their health problems, as well as stories of the health problems of their friends. As we slow down into their pace, we develop the patience of waiting that allows us to be present for and with them.

Patience gives us time to be available, and availability connects us with others. We can never experience the richness of empathy, the intimacy of shared joy and sorrow, or the solace of friendship without taking time to be available. There is no shortcut. Waiting gives us the chance to be open to each and every slowed-down opportunity.

Spiritual Practice: The Patience to Wait

> Do you have the patience to wait
> till your mud settles and the water is clear?
> Can you remain unmoving
> Till the right action arises by itself?[8]
> —Lao-tzu, *Tao Te Ching*

Meditate on this chapter's quotation about patience. After sitting with these words for a few minutes, write a prayer asking God for patience in whatever you are waiting for at this time in your life.

Questions to Ponder
Patience means trusting there's no quick fix.
- What situation in your life is currently demanding that you wait?
- How is this waiting teaching you patience?
- What would you like to ask from God about your patience, or impatience?
- What wisdom would you pass along to a younger person about living with patience?

Patience invites us to trust the fullness of God's time.
- When have you experienced the fullness of God's time in your life?
- Did you ever receive a "no" that was a prelude to a far greater "yes"?
- How are you waiting for God?
- How is God waiting for you?

Patience opens us to active waiting.
- How have you been empowered by "active waiting"?
- Is there a situation in which you could wait more actively right now?
- What could you do to participate in the waiting more fully?

Patience gives us time to be available to others.
- Who is genuinely present and available to you in your life?
- How are you available to others?
- What obstacles get in the way of your availability?
- How are you available to God?
- How might waiting help you to be more available to others?

The Second Gift of Waiting:

Loss of Control

For those of us for whom staying in control is the ultimate achievement, loss of control seems like a perverse and rotten gift indeed. The release of control, though, can be an empowering spiritual step.

Not long ago, coming back from the East Coast, I was unexpectedly caught in severe weather. As we departed, the skies looked fine, but the situation changed dramatically an hour-and-a-half later. It was then that the pilot announced, "We're circling Milwaukee, which is presently experiencing extremely severe weather." A half hour later the pilot declared, "It is still too dangerous to land in Milwaukee, and we are running low on fuel. We'll have to go to an alternate city to land." By this time, it was clear that everything was out of control. Connecting flights became impossible. It was uncertain whether we'd even be able to get into Milwaukee that same day.

At that point, we all gave up. When we accepted that everything was in pandemonium, life got easier. As we sat on the tarmac in Michigan, people spoke kindly to one another and passed their cell phones back and forth so everyone could call home. People began telling stories of where they were headed, of their families and jobs. We became more than silent strangers. We surrendered to forces beyond our control . . . and found each other.

We need, in love, to practice only this:
letting each other go. For holding on
comes easily; we do not need to learn it. [1]
　　—Rainer Maria Rilke, "Requiem for a Friend"

LOSS OF CONTROL TEACHES US
TO DEPEND ON ONE ANOTHER.

Every one of us could describe where we were on the morning of September 11, 2001. September 11th was a wilderness time for the people of New York City and Washington, D.C., and for the whole United States.

A member of my church, Don Macomber, went to New York City in October of 2001 as a Red Cross volunteer. The debris from the World Trade Center was six or seven stories high, the air filled with ash. Don confided that he was keenly aware that human bodies were still trapped in the smoking wreckage. On his second day there, Don was assigned to be the driver of an emergency response vehicle that would be stationed at Respite One, at Ground Zero. His responsibility was to pick up food from a restaurant, warm it, and serve it to Ground Zero workers. Each day he served food to Port Authority Police, to firefighters and police from all over the country, to semi-truck drivers, and to city-sweeper drivers who were hauling and cleaning up debris.

Don's job was to help the helpers. He gave tangible meaning to the dictionary definition of respite: "an interval of relief." [2] He not only served food but also provided a place of rest and safety. As he ministered, he listened to stories, dozens and dozens of stories.

Blessedly, there were many acts of generosity and courage at Ground Zero. Don encountered men in huge, dirt-filled harnesses whose job it was to follow the search dogs looking for bodies. When the dogs sniffed a human being, these brave men followed those dogs to the ends of the earth and beneath the earth, time after time being lowered into cavernous holes that could have easily fallen in and killed them.

Don also fed the Telephone Exchange Building workers. This was a particularly hazardous place to be assigned because of the constant risk of explosion and collapse. When imminent danger loomed for these rescuers, three loud blasts would sound—often several times each night—to warn the workers to stop immediately.

One night Don went over to Respite One about 11:30 P.M. to get ready for his shift. When he entered the dining hall, there was no talking, no chatter, no sharing of stories at all. There was just silence . . . and then he heard, clear as a bell, a woman singing. One of the food servers stood high on a chair in the middle of those tired rescuers, singing "His Eye Is on the Sparrow."

September 11th was a time of rallying together, of pitching in, of witnessing everyone's contribution. That out-of-control and tragic day fostered an uncanny spirit of mutuality and dependence on one another.

Needing each other is an imperative of our faith. When Jesus commissioned his twelve disciples, "He ordered them to take nothing for their journey except a staff; no bread, no bag, no money in their belts; but to wear sandals and not to put on two tunics" (Mark 6:8-9). In other words, Jesus made the disciples dependent on the kindness and hospitality of others. Jesus purposely sent the disciples out so they would *have* to receive and recognize other people's gifts.

In our "you can do it" culture, it is easy to believe that we don't need help. We take pride when we don't have to ask for assistance. We like the fact that we've got the situation under control. But waiting for something over which we have no control can topple our illusions of self-sufficiency rapidly. Rather than seeing this as a blow to our independence and self-esteem, or as unwelcome chaos in our carefully crafted schedule, we can see it as a gift—the gift of realizing that we don't have to do everything by ourselves. We are not alone. When we let go of control, we have a chance to reach out and let other people in.

The next time you feel things are out of control—whether it's because your plans are thwarted by an unexpected delay, or because life throws a major crisis your way—stop for a moment and consider: How can I use this time, as Jesus suggested, to reach out and recognize other people's gifts? Think of depending on one another as a bridge that can take you to new territory of caring and connection.

LOSS OF CONTROL ALLOWS US TO SURRENDER TO GRIEF.

> When it was evening, there came a rich man from Arimathea, named Joseph, who was also a disciple of Jesus. He went to Pilate and asked for the body of Jesus; then Pilate ordered it to be given to him. So Joseph took the body and wrapped it in a clean linen cloth and laid it in his own new tomb, which he had hewn in the rock. He then rolled a great stone to the door of the tomb and went away. Mary Magdalene and the other Mary were there, sitting opposite the tomb.
> —Matthew 27:57-61
> *A reading for the end of Lent: Holy Saturday*

On Sunday, June 24, 2001, my husband and I walked into our beloved church, Redeemer United Church of Christ in Sussex, Wisconsin, and we knew immediately that something was wrong. There was a terrible hushedness, and people were huddled together, whispering in small groups. There were none of the usual smiles and hugs that greeted us on a Sunday morning. Within minutes, we learned what had happened. A much-loved elderly couple in our church, Sylvester and Vera Steele, had picked up a neighbor and fellow church member, Millie Colby, and were driving east on Highway K. As the light turned green at the intersection of Highway K and Highway 164, they proceeded through and were broadsided by a driver who failed to stop. Sylvester was killed on the spot. As the car spun around with intense impact,

Millie was thrown out the door, landing yards away in the middle of the asphalt. Vera remained slumped underneath the dashboard. Church members John and Sue Chapel had been driving close behind when this horrible accident took place. Sue got out of their car and, bending over Millie's body in the middle of the road, tried to stem the flow of blood coming from Millie's head. After the EMTs arrived and Millie had been taken to Froedert Hospital on the Flight for Life helicopter, Sue and John dazedly made their way to church. Sue, still traumatized by the unspeakable tragedy she had witnessed, tried to explain to the stunned congregation what had happened. We later learned that Millie died of internal injuries. There were two funerals the following week. Vera, still hospitalized with serious injuries, could not even attend her husband's funeral.

On that tragic morning, we found ourselves hollowed and yielding. There was nothing to do but to sit quietly, to grieve, to pray, and to wait. That day was like Holy Saturday, the day after the crucifixion. It was an exercise in loss of control—and a lesson in surrender.

I have often thought about Jesus' disciples and all of his loved ones and what it must have been like for them after his crucifixion. The Bible doesn't fill in many details. The Scripture from Matthew talks about Joseph of Arimathea asking Pilate for Jesus' body and then burying it in a tomb as the two Marys grieved nearby. Luke says of Holy Saturday, "they rested according to the commandment." What must have been going through the minds of those who loved Jesus on that sickening day?

Presbyterian pastor Stephen Doughty offers this observation:

> What ultimately emerges in the hours after the crucifixion is a
> wholly yielded community. This is a gathering of folk who have
> let go and possess no specific idea of what they will hold onto
> next. They do not force an answer, nor do they rush after some-
> thing to fill the void. In deep pain, the yielded community simply
> draws together and immerses itself in the awe-filled mystery.[3]

Most of us know what that kind of pain feels like because we've been there. We each have experienced tragedy on a national scale or on a personal scale. Our unique circumstances are different, but the not knowing and the silence and the handing it over to God feel the same.

When something unbearable happens, we are tempted to move on quickly, to get over it, to avoid dwelling on it. The pain is excruciating, and all we want is for it to pass. We think if we can just be strong enough, we can buck up and it will go away. The opposite is, in fact, true. To move on too quickly prevents us from learning the lessons of surrender and yielding. Moving on too quickly prevents us from honoring the depth of our loss and sorrow. We need to stop, to sit, to just *be*.

In his book *A Path with Heart*, Jack Kornfield recalls a man running from himself:

> At one meditation retreat, I encountered a man whose only child, a four-year-old girl, had died in an accident just a few months before. Because she died in a car he was driving, he was filled with guilt as well as grief. He had stopped working and turned to full-time spiritual practice for solace. When he came to this retreat, he had already been to other retreats, he had been blessed by a great swami, and he had taken vows with a holy nun from South India. At the retreat his meditation cushion looked like a nest. It was surrounded by crystals, feathers, rosaries, and pictures of various great gurus. Each time he sat he would pray to each of the gurus and chant and recite sacred mantras. All of this to heal himself, he said. But perhaps all of this was to ward off his grief. After a few days I asked him if he would be willing simply to sit, without all his sacred objects, without prayer or chanting or any other practice. The next time he came in and just sat. In five minutes he was crying. In ten minutes he was sobbing and wailing. He had finally let himself take the seat in the midst of his sorrow; he had finally, truly begun to grieve. . . .[4]

To surrender to grief is to open the door to healing and to invite someone to walk beside us and share our pain. To surrender is to acknowledge that we are part of something larger than that which we can control. To surrender is to admit our powerlessness and to open ourselves to God's light and love.

This kind of deep, healing surrender cannot happen if we are barreling along at our normal, hectic life pace. When our calendar is filled to the brim, and every hour is accounted for, there is no time or space for the reflective mysteries of life-restoring grief. When we can take the first step of surrendering to quiet waiting—for God, for grief, for grace—we take the first step toward healing.

LOSS OF CONTROL TEACHES US RESILIENCE.

On March 7, 2004, I happened to be the preacher at my church, Redeemer United Church of Christ. It was Lent, and I preached on spiritual surrender and the lessons of being hollowed out and yielding. I recalled to the congregation that terrible and tragic morning when we had lost Sylvester and Millie in the gruesome auto accident. I talked about the powerlessness of September 11th and Don Macomber's courageous service. Five days later, on the evening of March 12th, Redeemer United Church of Christ in Sussex, Wisconsin, burned to the ground. New lessons in surrender were yet to be learned.

It was a memorable and stunning night as members of the congregation watched helplessly while eighty-one firefighters from thirteen departments used 375,000 gallons of water trying to extinguish the blaze. The persevering firefighters were exhausted by morning, overwhelmed by fatigue and emotionally defeated. The charred remains looked like the city of London during the Blitz, a ghostly, burned-out shell. We were all in shock that a random electrical fire had destroyed the whole thing.

Two days after the Friday night fire, the congregation of Our Savior's Lutheran Church graciously invited us to use their building for Sunday worship. Every Redeemer United Church of Christ member we had ever laid eyes on was in attendance. We were all there, hundreds of us, stunned and grieving. We needed to talk to one another and to weep.

That first Sunday we didn't know where the bathrooms were at Our Savior's Lutheran. We couldn't find the coat racks. I had brought baked goods to have with coffee, but I didn't know where the church kitchen was. Months later, we are still nomads. We hold worship on the burned-out church site in a huge rented tent, or in the cafeteria of the local high school. The Church Council meets at the public library. We schedule other meetings at various far-flung, kind-hearted churches or at the small business park that has become the church office. We meet anywhere and everywhere—and we are still waiting.

The loss of our church has taught us resilience. We have learned to let go of our anxiety and to be patient. We have become more flexible than we ever could have imagined. There are many things we have learned to do without. Most of all, we have learned the difference between church building and church community. Our building is gone, but our community is strong.

Author Christina Baldwin says, "The gift of despair *[and I would add, the gift of waiting]* is that it offers us a process for making peace with what is and becoming comfortable with new perceptions."[5]

We at Redeemer United Church of Christ in Sussex, Wisconsin, have not lost perspective. At the end of January 2005, it was presumed that 280,000 people died in the tsunami in Southeast Asia. At the end of August 2005, Hurricane Katrina devastated New Orleans and the Gulf Coast. We at Redeemer United Church of Christ may have lost our church building, but we haven't lost our homes, or each other, or our loved ones, or our neighborhood, or our villages, or our country.

In her book about refugees, psychologist Mary Pipher says,

It is difficult to describe or even imagine the challenges of getting started in a new country. Imagine yourself dropped in downtown Rio de Janeiro or Khartoum with no money, no friends, and no understanding of how that culture works. Imagine you have six months to learn the language and everything you need to support your family. Of course, that isn't a fair comparison because you know that the earth is round, what a bank is, and how to drive a car. And you have most likely not been tortured or seen family members killed within the last few months.[6]

Refugees and immigrants have a great deal to teach us about resilience. Often uprooted from all that offers routine and comfort and delight, refugees know what it is to endure the dismantling of everything that is familiar and to wait many months, or years, for a new place to feel like home. If you can, spend some time with a person from another country who has recently settled in the United States. Pay special attention to what that person can teach you about resilience.

When we are forced to wait—either through hard losses or through much-anticipated transitions—we, too, experience the dismantling of all that is familiar. While we wait, we often find ourselves out of control. In fact, loss of control is a hallmark of waiting. Loss of control can be terrifying; it can unhinge us as we lose sight of everything that is tidy and predictable.

Very gradually, though, it becomes a little more bearable. First, we understand that we are not alone and that we can ask for help. Second, we sit and come to grips with all that we have lost. Finally, we name and claim all that we have navigated and survived—and we can celebrate our resilience.

Spiritual Practice: A Reflection on Finding Your Way

"What to Do in the Darkness"

Go slowly
Consent to it
But don't wallow in it
Know it as a place of germination
And growth
Remember the light
Take an outstretched hand if you find one
Exercise unused senses
Find the path by walking it
Practice trust
Watch for dawn[7]
      —Marilyn Chandler McEntyre

Meditate on this poem. How does it speak to your experience?
Create your own list of "What to Do in the Darkness."

Questions to Ponder
Loss of control teaches us to depend on one another.
- Think of a time when you were in a crisis. What gifts did you
  witness in others? How did each person's contribution make a
  difference?
- What contribution did you make? How did that change the
  situation? If you found yourself in the same situation again,
  would you do anything differently?
- Can you think of a time when waiting helped you to reach out
  to others?

Loss of control allows us to surrender to grief.
- Think of a time when you surrendered to circumstances you
  couldn't control. What was that like for you?
- Is there an area of your life where loss of control might have
  some things to teach you?

- Is there any grief or loss you need to name and sit with?
- How might you bring the need to surrender to your prayer?

Loss of control teaches us resilience.
- Christina Baldwin says, "The gift of despair is that it offers us a process for making peace with what is and becoming comfortable with new perceptions."[8] Describe a situation where these words have been true for you.
- Think of a situation where a forced wait made you realize that you were not in control. What did you learn from that experience about resilience?
- What has waiting taught you about resilience?

The Third Gift of Waiting:
Living in the Present

Waiting teaches us to dwell fully where we are. When we can't control our circumstances and we can't predict the future, we have the opportunity to live in the present.

Sometimes after a huge Milwaukee blizzard, while we're waiting for the roads to be shoveled, we hear the news that schools will be closed and that everyone who can should stay home and off the highways. What a gift this news is! I can cancel my hard-nosed plans. I can go back to bed. I can write a few checks I meant to get to yesterday. I can make cookies with the kids. I can watch the movie from the video store that I rented three days ago. I can live in the present moment.

> *When the Buddha was asked, "Sir, what do you and your monks practice?" he replied, "We sit, we walk, and we eat." The questioner continued, "But sir, everyone sits, walks, and eats," and the Buddha told him, "When we sit, we know we are sitting. When we walk, we know we are walking. When we eat, we know we are eating."*[1]
>
> —Thich Nhat Hanh, *Living Buddha, Living Christ*

LIVING IN THE PRESENT CALLS US TO "BE HERE NOW."
In her amazing autobiography of self-insight and endurance, poet
Lucy Grealy describes her childhood cancer and her lifelong dis-
figurement. Having undergone dozens of surgeries, Grealy spent
much of her life waiting. When she was a child, she endured chemotherapy for two-and-a-half years. While waiting to see her
doctor, she found that the time would pass more quickly if she
meandered down the corridor to the clinic's bathroom. In the first
stall, someone had scratched graffiti onto the door that said, "God
is near." In the second stall, the same person had scratched, "Be
here now." During her years of chemotherapy, Lucy pondered
these two messages, both of which she sensed might offer her
some important truth. She writes in her memoir:

> *Be Here Now.* I didn't want to be here now. My wanting was
> inconsequential. I *was* here now, whether I liked it or not. But
> something about this saying attracted me, either despite or
> because of its seeming simplicity, and two out of three times I
> went for door number two.[2]

Be here now. This admonition asks us to live intentionally in the
present, to focus on what is happening now. It invites us to pay
attention and to learn from our current circumstances. It invites
us to forget about our waiting, to willingly be distracted by the
present. *Be here now* invites us to *enjoy* the moment. This technique
really works! Next time you are stuck in traffic or waiting in line,
give it a try. Look around. Start noticing what you see, hear, and
feel. You might be surprised by something funny or interesting or
revealing—even about yourself!

LIVING IN THE PRESENT INVITES US
TO RELINQUISH WORRY.
Etty Hillesum, a young Dutchwoman and law student, and one
of the world's most heroic diarists of the Holocaust, tried her best

to be a comfort to fellow sufferers and to put worry aside. The degree of stress in Amsterdam's Jewish community in the early 1940s was almost unimaginable. While Etty waited for years with thousands of other Jews as they were stripped of freedoms month by month, and then eventually shipped off to concentration camps to be gassed, she aspired to retain hope, to live in gratitude, and to live in the present moment. She worked fervently on the Jewish Council, advocating for her fellow Jews, and then, for the rest of the time, tried to serve as a nonanxious and generous presence. Etty Hillesum knew what was happening around her as Hitler took over Holland, yet she chose to appreciate beauty, to savor friendship, and to live in the present. One day Etty spent time reading Matthew 6:34: "So do not worry about tomorrow, for tomorrow will bring worries of its own. Today's trouble is enough for today." After reading this Scripture, she wrote in her journal:

> We have to fight them daily, like fleas, those many small worries about the morrow, for they sap our energies. We make mental provisions for the days to come, and everything turns out differently, quite differently. Sufficient unto the day. The things that have to be done must be done, and for the rest we must not allow ourselves to become infested with thousands of petty fears and worries, so many motions of no confidence in God. . . . Ultimately we have just one moral duty: to reclaim large areas of peace in ourselves, more and more peace, and to reflect it toward others. . . .[3]

The longer I live, the more I believe that worry is an utterly unprofitable and ineffective condition. Yet worry is a pervasive condition—especially when we are waiting for something important, such as a test result, a mortgage approval, a job decision, news about a loved one. The truth is, worry never teaches us anything useful. When we worry, we disempower ourselves and lessen our trust in God. When we worry, our anxiety mounts as we manipulate everyone around us to make room for our worry and to accommodate our anxiety.

Waiting presents us with a unique opportunity to shift gears from useless worry about the future to engagement in the present. What is good right now? What can I be at peace with today? Living in the present invites us to make the spiritual leap of trusting in God, believing that God is always near.

LIVING IN THE PRESENT ALLOWS US TO SAY, "IT IS ENOUGH."

Most of us live as if God were on vacation and we are in charge, as if the planet's daily spinning depended on our relentless productivity, on our holding up our end of the bargain. We worry how we are going to handle everything that is on our plate. The truth is, we function much better when we are able to turn our endless work over to God. Sometimes, thankfully, our schedules get interrupted by something for which we have to wait. Something holds us up or stops us in our tracks. When we can take this moment to step back, we can gain some perspective.

Three summers ago, when my mom was living with us before and after her colon cancer surgery, the days were demanding. I was waiting for my mom to heal and to feel confident enough to return to her own home. I was doing my job, anxiously worrying whether her cancer was metastasizing, taking care of the kids, fixing meals, doing laundry, and sometimes commuting to the hospital twice a day. I was conscious over and over of all that constantly remained undone. I finally realized I needed to stop. I needed to stop trying to take care of everything, to stop worrying. I needed to reclaim an area of peace within myself. I needed to recognize what was "sufficient unto the day." I needed to declare, "It is enough. This is all that is possible." Over and over in the midst of the clamor, I had to admit my own powerlessness, to relinquish worry, and to trust God. When I did that, I could breathe more easily, offer up my worry, and allow God to help. Loosening my grip and living more lightly allowed me to take a walk each morning, to relax a little in the evening, and even to experience a good night's sleep.

"It is enough." A small, simple treasure. Consider it the next time waiting makes you crabby or anxious or stressed out. Maybe waiting is offering you a chance to receive this empowering gift.

LIVING IN THE PRESENT TEACHES US TO BE FAITHFUL IN SMALL THINGS.

One of my favorite Scriptures has always been the Easter evening story of the disciples on the road to Emmaus. In the twenty-fourth chapter of Luke, two weary and grief-stricken disciples were plodding along. Jesus had just been crucified, and their dream of the Messiah who would redeem Israel had been wrecked. Then a stranger joined them on the road and innocently began asking details of this sorry tale. As the two disciples approached the village of Emmaus, their obligation to hospitality kicked in, and they said, "Come on in, it's getting dark; stay with us and eat." It was at the supper table that the stranger revealed who he was. When Jesus took the bread, blessed it, broke it, and gave it to them, they finally recognized him.

I have always found this story intriguing. It is amazing—and yet not so amazing—that Jesus revealed himself in the breaking of the bread, around the supper table, doing something ordinary. We are all revealed to be our true selves at the "supper table"—not at the table *per se* but in all that is ordinary, in all that is daily, and in all that is routine. It is in the middle of the commonplace, the tedious, and the mundane that our true colors show. We can all be shining heroes and heroines once in a while, but it is in the tiresome trenches of routine that faithfulness matters.

Theologian Elizabeth Dreyer has written, "You never have to go to Lent. Lent always comes to you."[4] This statement is profound. This statement changes all of life. This statement says that ministry is everywhere, that faithfulness is everywhere.

And it comes back to *living in the present*. Living in the present is an invitation to sit down, take a deep breath, and ask, "What is in front of my face this very minute that summons me to faithfulness?"

That summons is most likely found in everyday routines. Maybe it means not going ballistic when a husband brings home two pounds of shredded cheese rather than the two cans of cheddar cheese soup you had so carefully instructed. Maybe it means waiting that forty-five minutes in the school parking lot for a child to return from an out-of-town game without anger and impatience. Maybe it means listening with empathy and containment to a ninety-five-year-old relative who has already told us three times about what happened last week in line at the bank.

Everyday faithfulness means helping others feel safe and secure. It means showing up at school or at the nursing home. It is in the saying good-bye and the saying goodnight. It is in the praying at mealtimes or in the packing of lunches or in the matching of socks.

Several years ago I was in New Mexico at a Presbyterian Conference Center called Ghost Ranch. There I met a wonderful, warm, centered person named Gail who emanated a gentle self-confidence and an unshakable faith in God. She told us that when she was a little girl, her parents hung a sign on the footboard of her bed that read:

> MOM AND DAD LOVE GAIL.
> GOD LOVES GAIL.

Can you imagine the good vibrations that must have come sailing out from the foot of that bed? Every night Gail was tucked into bed, she could look down and absorb that triumphant message of unconditional love. When I returned home to Wisconsin, I was determined to offer my own children the gift of those affirming words. Every night for four years, I trotted up to their rooms and bestowed on them a benediction before bed:

> MOM AND DAD LOVE DAVID.
> GOD LOVES DAVID.
> MOM AND DAD LOVE KATIE.
> GOD LOVES KATIE.

It became a routine, a routine that once in while even I, who was formerly so inspired, had little energy for. Some nights I had to drag myself up those stairs to confer my spent and overtired blessing. But then, lo and behold, not long ago I was out of town leading a retreat, and I found a piece of paper stuck in my purse, a piece of paper from my daughter, Kate. The wrinkled paper read:

KATIE AND DAVID AND DAD LOVE MOM.
GOD LOVES MOM.

Recently, my sophisticated and rather cynical young adult son said out of the blue as he packed his lunch, "You know that thing you say to us every night, Mom? I want that on my tombstone."

Glory be! Who would ever have believed it? The littlest things really do count.

And that is the secret gift of waiting: an invitation not only to pay attention to the little things, but to see what needs to be done, and to be faithful in saying yes. Waiting invites us to recognize Jesus and his call to faithfulness in the most ordinary moments of life.

Spiritual Practice: A "Living in the Present" Exercise

Are you a habitual "waiter?" How much of your life do you spend waiting? What I call "small-scale waiting" is waiting in line at the post office, in a traffic jam, at the airport, or waiting for someone to arrive, to finish work, and so on. "Large-scale waiting" is waiting for the next vacation, for a better job, for the children to grow up, for a truly meaningful relationship, for success, to make money, to be important, to become enlightened. It is not uncommon for people to spend their whole life waiting to start living.[5]

—Eckhart Tolle

Reflect on this quotation about waiting. How does it apply to your life? Ponder a while and then write a prayer for yourself.

Questions to Ponder

Living in the present calls us to "be here now."
- Say the words: "Be here now." What insight do these words offer you in your present circumstances?
- Think of a place you have to go this week where you know you will need to wait. What could you do to practice "being here now" while you wait? Try it and note what effect it has on you and on those around you.

Living in the present invites us to relinquish worry.
- What are you most worried about right now? What could you do to surrender this worry today?
- What do you need from God?

Living in the present allows us to say, "It is enough."
- Say the words "It is enough." How do you feel?
- Where might you incorporate the practice of saying "It is enough" this week?

Living in the present teaches us to be faithful in small things.
- How does your experience of waiting call you to notice the small things?
- Is there any specific act of everyday faithfulness that you could offer to another this week?

The Fourth Gift of Waiting:

Compassion

When we are waiting for something important in our lives, we tend to seek out others who will understand our restlessness and anxieties. Think of the Advent story of Mary and her cousin Elizabeth, one young woman and one much older woman, both pregnant. They were both living in circumstances beyond their control, expecting an unexpected child, and in their fear and excitement they reached out to one another. Their shared waiting gave them a unique understanding of what each was going through, and they could embrace each other in compassion.

We, too, know the feeling of waiting with others, in uncertainty, in crisis. Maybe you've had the experience of waiting in the family members' lounge of the hospital intensive care unit. If so, you know the feeling of desperation and intense anxiety. You know the feeling of talking to a stranger sitting next to you and asking that person who their loved one is and what they are waiting for. You know the feeling of a stranger coming up to you and saying, "I'm going down to the cafeteria. Do you want to come? Can I bring you something back?" Even with total strangers, sharing fears and insecurities while we wait offers a bridge of understanding.

Waiting together in uncertainty creates compassion.

A
Hunting party
Sometimes has a greater chance
Of flushing love and God
Out into the open
Than a warrior
All
Alone.[1]
—Hafiz, fourteen-century Sufi master

COMPASSION REMINDS US THAT WE ARE NOT ALONE.
A thirty-seven-year-old woman has been struggling with metastasizing breast cancer for two years. When she was breastfeeding her newborn baby, she discovered she had a lump in her breast. She is currently waiting for a new round of radiation treatments to be over. I called her the other night for an update on her progress. Instead of being filled with self-pity and despair, she spoke of gratitude. "I counted them up," she said. "There are over a hundred people who are helping me: praying for me, bringing my family food, providing me with rides to my doctors' appointments, filling in for me at work, babysitting my children. I can't believe all these people care about me." In the midst of waiting to be healed, Carla knows she does not wait alone but is surrounded by compassion.

Years ago when my husband and I were in our thirties, he became gravely ill with an endocrine illness called Cushing's Disease. It was a taxing time of waiting: waiting for one medical test after another; waiting to see if any treatment would be effective. Our children were small, and it was hard to find time for grocery shopping and work and daily chores while he was in the hospital. One afternoon I walked out from the church I pastored and got in my car to pick up the kids from daycare. Astonishingly enough, the back seat was filled with food! Enough to last at least a week! One of my parishioners, knowing that I was having a difficult time keeping everything together, had cooked and cooked so that I would not have to. My load suddenly lightened. I sat behind the wheel and cried. This friend's act of compassion relieved my anxiety and came as a grace-filled and welcome relief.

We all yearn for someone to be with us in the hard times. When my niece Lydia was born, I gave her a little velvet-covered photo book titled *People Who Love Me*. Over the years my sister, Heather, her mother, has been patiently filling the album with snapshots of Lydia's relatives and loved ones. Heather was awakened in the middle of night by the sound of a slamming drawer. She got up to see what was wrong and found her three-year-old daughter sitting up in bed, paging through a book illumined only by her nightlight.

"Honey, what's the matter? Are you having trouble sleeping?"

"Oh, Mommy," Lydia replied, "when I'm afraid, this helps me feel better."

Lydia had gotten her *People Who Love Me* book out of the drawer where she knew it would be. In her waiting to go back to sleep, Lydia had surrounded herself with her own little cloud of witnesses who assured her of their love.

In her work with chronically ill and dying patients, Dr. Rachel Naomi Remen is sometimes called in the middle of the night by family members who are frightened and need reassurance. Most often the family members simply need to know that what their loved one is experiencing is normal. Dr. Remen writes:

> The women who call at night are always speaking from the heart. In the beginning when I was a pediatrician, the women would call about the children. But my scope has broadened. Now the women call about their partners, their sisters, their friends. Their voices are sometimes weary, sometimes sad, almost always anxious. They are looking for someone to wait with them.[2]

The anxiety of waiting breaks down our usual barriers and opens us to the compassion of others. People we haven't seen in weeks may surface to offer just what we need. The reverse is also true: Waiting stretches our usual boundaries and opens us to opportunities to connect with others in compassion. We may hear of someone who is waiting in pain and feel called to go out of our way to do something special for them.

When we share the suffering of those who wait—and they with us—we know we are not waiting alone. This is what compassion—from the Latin *cum*, meaning "with," and *passio*, meaning "suffering"—is all about.

COMPASSION TEACHES US TO RECEIVE.

As a child, I was raised with the admonition, "It is more blessed to give than to receive." Most of all, I was brought up learning never to be "beholden." To be beholden was a nasty state of affairs in which I might lose the moral high ground and be constantly owing someone else. I was raised to be an excellent and generous giver, but a dreadful and graceless receiver.

When my husband was diagnosed with Cushing's, the doctors searched for months before finally discovering the culprit tumor in one of his lungs. Immediately after surgery, as I sat waiting in the intensive care unit, a hospital chaplain came and asked if she might keep me company and offer some support. I hastily replied, "Thank you, but no. I'll be okay. I've been a hospital chaplain myself, you know."

She looked at me kindly and said, "Let me help you. It's different when it's a member of your own family." She took my arm, and we went into my husband's room. I was stunned. There he was, white as death, indistinguishable from a corpse, hooked up to every tube imaginable. I choked and sobbed and leaned into the hospital chaplain. I said, "Thank you for staying. I didn't realize I needed help so badly."

One of the early Christian Middle Eastern monastics, Abba James, once said, "It is better to receive hospitality than to offer it."[3]

Now that's something to ponder! This admonition varies a great deal from what many of us have been taught.

In the Gospel of John, chapter 13, Jesus was getting ready for Passover, what we have come to know as the Last Supper. He took a bowl of water and untied a towel from around his waist as he prepared to wash his disciples' feet. As he made his way around to Peter, Peter declared, "You will never wash my feet." Jesus answered, "Unless I wash you, you have no share with me."

Jesus reminds us that we have no share with anyone unless we learn to receive.[4] If we cannot receive, we will never empower those who would offer their gifts in compassion. If we cannot receive, we will never treat others as our equals. If we cannot receive, we can never fully understand compassion.

When we find ourselves in a period of waiting—especially if we are waiting for something important in our lives—we have new occasions to learn the gift of receiving. Being able to receive comfortably and with grace is a blessed relief.

COMPASSION ALLOWS US TO BE SEEN FOR WHO WE REALLY ARE.

One night, John, my ER doctor husband, came home from work quite elated. He had been just about to enter a female patient's room when he noticed a sign on the door that said, "Hindi translator needed." There was little chance in this urban Milwaukee hospital that a Hindi translator was suddenly going to materialize, but he strolled on in. He saw a young Indian couple sitting together. The husband, a graduate student, greeted him in English, and my husband asked, "Where is your wife from?"

The young man replied, "We're from Chhattisgarh. You would never have heard of it."

My husband turned to the woman and said in Chhattisgarhi—since Hindi was his first language—"I'm from Bisrampur," and named the two other villages of Bitalpur and Simga that are on the local bus route in this impossibly remote place. John continued asking in Chhattisgarhi, "Where do you hurt?" and the young woman burst into tears. She was stunned and amazed to hear a six-foot-six-inch American doctor speaking her own local language and understanding where her home was.

We all need to be seen and heard.

Life coach Dr. Martha Beck illustrates what it feels like to be seen:

> . . . I know one woman who survived an emotionally barren childhood on the strength of one fleeting encounter with a person whose name she never knew. "I was about four," Chloe recalls, "and my father had taken me to his office for some reason. There was a secretary there who reacted to me in a way I'd never experienced. Her whole being seemed to light up when she saw me. I think she was just one of those people who loves all children. While my dad went into his office, this woman came over to me and crouched down, so our eyes were level. I can't recall what she said. But while she talked, she looked straight into my eyes. I couldn't remember anyone ever doing this before. And I remember feeling, all the way through my body, "She *sees* me!"[5]

During the frustration of waiting, we may feel invisible and powerless. We may lose confidence that we can make ourselves understood. Out of desperation, we may seek out someone who will truly see us. Or we may be fortunate enough to have someone reach out to us. And, suddenly, everything shifts. Instead of being a huge drain of our energy, waiting becomes a receiving pool where compassion collects and overflows.

Little do we suspect the gifts available to us in the murky waters of waiting. Much can we receive through the in-"sight" of compassionate friends. When another person reaches out to us with compassion and truly sees us, it is an enormous grace. In Dr. Remen's words, "The places in which we are seen and heard are holy places."[6]

COMPASSION HELPS US GATHER STRENGTH FROM OTHERS. One of the most courageous books I have ever read about waiting is hostage negotiator Terry Waite's memoir *Taken on Trust*, his account of four years of solitary confinement in Beirut. Terry Waite was the Assistant for Anglican Communion Affairs under Archbishop Runcie. He often negotiated the international release of hostages on behalf of the Anglican Church. In the midst of negotiation, he was held hostage himself from 1987 to 1991. Once while his captors forced him to be chained in a fetal position, he comforted himself by remembering heroic and famous prisoners whom he had met or read about: Alexander Solzhenitsyn, Arthur Koestler, Desmond Tutu. He gained strength knowing he was part of this far-reaching and indomitable community of suffering and endurance.

Though our waiting does not make international headlines, we still know what it is like to feel solidarity with others who wait. When I ask the question, "Who in my life waits the most faithfully alongside those who suffer?" I would have to answer immediately that it is my friend and colleague Marilyn Hair. Marilyn Hair, her husband, Rick Steele, and I were all students together at Yale Divinity School back in the seventies. In 1983, when my husband, John, and I moved to Milwaukee, we were all, amazingly enough, reunited. We ended up living near the same big avenue, about one mile apart. I gave birth to our second child, Katie, in December of 1983. Rick and Marilyn gave birth to their first child, Sarah, in December of 1984. Marilyn's life changed at that moment, for it was at that time that she began to lay down her life for another.

In April of 1985, Sarah was diagnosed with a disease called FOP: *fibrodysplasia ossificans progressiva*. This condition is referred to as "stone man deformity" and essentially causes a second skeleton to grow in the skeletal muscles until the entire body becomes petrified like a fossil. This petrification takes places over time as the young person bumps himself or herself and develops swellings and painful lesions. Bumps and bruises cause enough trauma to create bony growth. In other words, bruises can cause extra bones.

When Sarah was a baby and a toddler, I remember her mother trying to pad everything in sight. She hoped against hope that if she could prevent Sarah from bumping herself, the ossification would slow down. She bumper-padded the crib and made pillows for the back of the high chair, the piano bench, even the baby gate. She wouldn't let Sarah ride in my car because it was not sufficiently padded. But eventually, despite Marilyn's best efforts, Sarah's body became petrified due to this extra bone growth.

Today Sarah excels academically and is able to do her school-work by nudging a dowel stick on her computer keyboard. She lives in a Permobil power wheelchair and is hoisted into bed at night by a pulley that lowers her in place. She can talk and can take in small bits of softened food but has movement only in her fingers, which are permanently fixed at her chin. She needs twenty-four-hour assistance in turning her head, rolling over in bed, eating, using the toilet, bathing, dressing, or scratching an itch.

Marilyn's life has changed more than she ever could have imagined when we were young and carefree back in seminary. She has had to retire from being a United Methodist pastor in order to care for Sarah, but she has miraculously turned being "Sarah's mother" into a vocation of personal caregiving and public service for those affected by this disease.

In an article titled "Bridging the Challenges: The Effects of FOP on the Family," Marilyn wrote:

I have learned compassion. There is a lot of pain in the world. I have a colleague in the pastoral ministry who was praised by his parishioners as an exceptional preacher, teacher, and admin-istrator. His only shortcoming, they claimed, was that he had not suffered and he could not fully identify with their suffering. Then his wife was diagnosed with breast cancer while she was pregnant with their [second] child. Now he has suffered; now he understands. Suffering changes a person. I would even suggest that there are two kinds of people in the world; those who have suffered and those who have not. . . . My family and I belong to the "community of those who bear the mark of pain." There are some advantages to belonging to this group. Suffering makes us struggle and reflect about what we believe and what life means. This struggle can make us richer, deeper people. . . .[7]

Marilyn has served on the International Fibrodysplasia Ossificans Progressiva Assocation's Board of Directors for ten years. She has been a tireless interpreter and fundraiser. She has appeared on national, regional, and local television, including the show 20/20 and a Discovery Health special called "Medical Incredible." She has written speeches and sermons and has conducted seminars. She has composed brilliant and insightful journal articles. Through her advocacy for persons with FOP, she has created a haven of empathy and connection. She has assured members of a suffering and fragile community that they are not alone. She waits with them, offering hope and compassion.

When we find ourselves waiting, we may feel as if we are on an isolated island, cut off from the rest of the world. The true gift of waiting, however, is not isolation but connection. Intense waiting opens the door to even more intense love. Waiting creates a unique bond among those who experience it together. It is a breeding ground for compassion; it nurtures the seeds of strength. Waiting can be a lonely time, but waiting can also draw us out. It allows us to reach out, and to be reached to. When we know that others share our frustrations and struggles, we feel less isolated. We can exchange encouragement, empathy, and survival skills as we navigate our journeys together.

COMPASSION OFFERS US HOPE.

While waiting may initially feel as if someone has closed all the doors, waiting actually gives other people an opportunity to nudge those doors open with their compassion, bringing with them the gift of hope. Through their eyes and actions, we can see things as we hadn't seen them before. Through their compassion, we can feel a renewed sense of hope.

Author and minister Victor Parachin tells the story of a visiting teacher who brought this very gift to a long-hospitalized young boy.

A school system in a large city had a special program to help hospitalized children keep up with their school work. One day, a teacher who worked in the program received a routine call asking her to visit such a child. She was given the child's name, hospital, and room number. Her instructions were to help the boy with lessons in grammar.

That same day, the teacher went to see the boy. No one mentioned to her that the youth had been badly burned and was in great pain. Caught off guard by the boy's disfiguring burns, his bandaged face and his obvious physical pain, she struggled through the lesson. When she left the hospital room, the teacher was disappointed with herself and felt she had not accomplished much with her hospitalized student.

However, upon returning the next day, a nurse asked her: "What did you do with that boy? Ever since you visited yesterday, his attitude toward recovery has improved." The teacher was surprised and listened carefully as the nurse explained that the entire staff was worried about the youth. He had not been responding effectively to treatment nor was he showing much improvement. "After your visit he became more responsive to treatment. It's as though he's decided to live," the nurse explained.

The explanation for the boy's remarkable transformation came two weeks later when the boy quietly said that he had completely given up hope until the teacher arrived. Everything changed when he came to a simple realization which he expressed this way: "They wouldn't send a teacher to work with me on grammar if I was dying, would they?"[8]

The enemy of hope—despair—may creep in uninvited, bearing heavy burdens. But hope shines radiantly through the embrace of our friends. That's how it is with God's compassion, too. God's abiding love seeks us out and finds us wherever we are. What a blessing this is! We always have a future with God because in life or in death there is no place we can escape from God's love. God loves us anywhere we could possibly be. Hear these words from Psalm 139:

> Where can I go then from your Spirit?
>> where can I flee from your presence?
> If I climb up to heaven, you are there;
>> if I make the grave my bed, you are there also.
> If I take the wings of the morning
>> and dwell in the uttermost parts of the sea,
> Even there your hand will lead me
>> and your right hand hold me fast.[9]

When we enter a critical waiting period—whether it's waiting for life-changing news, such as word about a new job, or a potentially life-threatening report, such as a medical test result—we enter new territory. While it may initially appear as a dry desert, it can be as surprising as a desert coming into spring bloom, with subtle gifts and vibrant signs of life. As we walk the path of waiting, compassion sprouts around us, filled with possibilities of hope. Hope changes the landscape from barren to blossoming. Hope gives us something to hold on to. Hope preserves the future.

Waiting teaches us the value of hope.

Spiritual Practice: Heart to Heart

Step One. Picture God's heart.

Step Two. Ask yourself: What am I holding in my heart these days? How does this feel?

Step Three. Think of others who may be experiencing what you are experiencing. Connect your heart with their hearts.

Step Four. Bring all of this into God's heart. Allow yourself to feel compassion.[10]

Questions to Ponder

Compassion reminds us that we are not alone.

• How would you define the word *compassion?*

• Think of a recent time when someone came along beside you while you waited. What did they do to let you know they were "with you"? How did you feel?

Compassion teaches us to receive.

• Do you struggle over receiving help? What are some things that are especially hard for you to receive?

• Think of a time when you were able to receive help gracefully. How did that affect the giver? How did it affect you? What did you learn from that experience?

• How might waiting help you to be able to receive?

Compassion allows us to be seen for who we really are.

• Who in your life really sees you? What difference does this make?

• How might waiting lead you to see, or be seen, more honestly?

Compassion helps us gather strength from others.

• With whom have you experienced a particular bond as a result of waiting together? How do you benefit from this relationship?

- What are you waiting for at this time in your life? Can you imagine how this period of waiting might create a link of compassion with someone else?

Compassion offers us hope.
- When has hope been a gift in your life?
- What are your sources of hope?
- How might you offer hope to another person this week?

The Fifth Gift of Waiting:

Gratitude

I hate waiting in line at the grocery store—but sometimes I see my full cart and am grateful I can afford this food. When I think of the people whom this food will feed, I am grateful for my family and the companionship at our table.

Waiting can give us unexpected moments to be grateful for everything that is peaceful or lovely or running smoothly, the small things we may not have noticed before. Waiting can inspire us to look around carefully and to observe what's there. Yes, we are waiting. But look at all these people who are offering help. Yes, we are waiting. But aren't we lucky we're going through this now rather than ten years ago?

Waiting teaches us to appreciate those pieces of our lives that have gracefully fallen into place. Waiting teaches us gratitude.

If the only prayer you say in your entire life is "Thank you," that would suffice.[1]
—Meister Eckhart, German mystic (1260– c.1329)

GRATITUDE TURNS OBSTACLES INTO OPPORTUNITY.

When Jesus saw the crowds, he went up the mountain; and after he sat down, his disciples came to him. Then he began to speak, and taught them, saying:
Blessed are the poor in spirit, for theirs is the kingdom of heaven.
Blessed are those who mourn, for they will be comforted.
Blessed are the meek, for they will inherit the earth.
Blessed are those who hunger and thirst for righteousness, for they will be filled.
Blessed are the merciful, for they will receive mercy.
Blessed are the pure in heart, for they will see God.
Blessed are the peacemakers, for they will be called children of God.
Blessed are those who are persecuted for righteousness' sake, for theirs is the kingdom of heaven.
Blessed are you when people revile you and persecute you and utter all kinds of evil against you falsely on my account. Rejoice and be glad, for your reward is great in heaven, for in the same way they persecuted the prophets who were before you.
—The Beatitudes, Matthew 5:1-12

A number of years ago, I was sharing with a friend that I was going through a period of feeling blue, of feeling depressed. I told my friend I was usually a very "up," enthusiastic, positive person, and that this depression was awkward and uncomfortable, and was wearing me down.

Much to my amazement, my friend asked me, "Can you look at this period of depression as a messenger who is trying to tell you something? Can you regard this depression as a gift from which you might gain some new understanding or some new insight?"

Given the way I was feeling, it was very hard to imagine depression as a positive messenger or, even more ludicrously, as a gift. I had always regarded depression as something to be warded off at all costs. I went home that day and asked myself if there were a possibility that I could look at this depression differently. Was this an opportunity for me to change something, an opportunity to grow? I thought of Christina Baldwin's great line, "Life is a great unending opportunity to see things differently, to keep reframing disaster and discouragement into faith."[2] It got me thinking about reframing.

Our living room walls are covered with pictures. These are not ordinary pictures, but framed mementos from all over the world: wondrous, but simple handmade items purchased at little cost. In our collection is a small, one-hundred-year-old quilt bought on the streets of New Delhi, a ninety-eight-cent clay necklace from a bazaar in Mexico, a carved wooden fan from Beijing. For years I have taken my foreign excursion treasures over to Ed at You Frame It. Ed is a master reframer. He eyeballs a piece, and he instantly sees it transformed. He imagines the frame color, the mat color, ascertains whether it should be double-matted, and what the dimensions of the shadow box should be. Presto. The ninety-eight-cent clay necklace becomes a masterpiece. I am always amazed. Framed and shadowboxed, these beloved collectibles look as if they could be hanging in a museum.

In the Beatitudes Jesus offers us the chance to be in the reframing business. Many of the persons described in the Beatitudes, says well-known preacher Fred Craddock, "are victims, to be sure, but the beatitudes deliver them from a victim mentality."[3] The Beatitudes invite us to see blessedness even in the midst of tumult and suffering. They invite us not to be trapped by circumstances, but to look for the grace, to find the possibilities, to explore the edges for growth.

The ultimate example of reframing is the Easter Story—for what are the Beatitudes about if not seeing resurrection in the midst of crucifixion? Is there any greater example of reframing than Jesus' transformation from tortured death to empty tomb? Each time we read the Beatitudes, they encourage us to live as people who believe in Easter, as reframers of life.

If the ultimate reframe is Easter, perhaps the most mundane reframe is waiting. But the Beatitudes teach us that we are blessed in our waiting because it is then that we have the opportunity to see with new eyes, to count our blessings. I do not believe that God clobbers us over the head with suffering or waiting so we'll learn from them, but I do believe God blesses us with insight when life circumstances put us on hold.

The next time you are feeling blocked by waiting, stand back a little from your victimizing circumstances and try looking at the picture with new eyes. Reframe it and see what you can come up with. Try using the Beatitude methodology to be grateful in all things, including your waiting. Ask, "What opportunities for new understanding, for growth, are available to me? What am I grateful for even in these tough times?"

GRATITUDE MOVES US BEYOND ENTITLEMENT.

Have you ever been with people who believe they deserve to go through life first-class? These are the folks who demand the best seats, the best healthcare, the corner office with the best view. They go through life with a chip on their shoulders feeling deprived if they are not elevated beyond the common rabble. They often act needy and greedy, and always insist on special attention. Debbie Ford writes:

> A lot of our conclusions about life keep us stuck in a state of entitlement. When we are viewing life through the lens of entitlement, we cannot receive our gifts. . . . Entitlement hides the lens of gratitude and shuts down our appreciation of the everyday miracles of life.[4]

We are all easily tempted by entitlement, especially when we are stressed. Entitlement is particularly seductive when we are waiting because we tend to feel sorry for ourselves. We say, "Look at my anxiety. Look at my misery. Look at my distress. I deserve a leg up." It is very easy to become whiny, to expect special privileges, and to act entitled while we are waiting. In the pain of our waiting, we may slip into feeling entitled. But entitlement defeats gratitude. Entitlement is a continual comparing, insisting on getting more than someone else. If we believe that we are getting less than we deserve, there is no way we will be content, let alone grateful.

The next time you find yourself waiting impatiently and feeling that you deserve better, pause. Your waiting is offering you a choice: Bemoan your circumstances or be grateful for your blessings. Remember what is going well. Breathe in a little gratitude.

GRATITUDE OPENS OUR EYES TO THE BLESSINGS OF SMALL THINGS.

The feeling of Gratitude is a shy bird. Chasing it does no good. Genuine Gratitude can never be forced. Trying hard to feel Gratitude is like trying hard to fall asleep or fall in love. The harder you try to be grateful, the more elusive the experience becomes. It must come to you, on its own schedule and on its own terms. You practice Gratitude by carefully building a home in your heart to accommodate it. The bird does not always come, but if you make a home for it, it comes often enough.[5]

—Timothy Miller, *How to Want What You Have*

When we are waiting, we are vulnerable—and our hearts are open. Therein lies the gift: Our open hearts teach us to notice the blessings of small things we would have never noticed before. In our fragility and brokenness, little things become a lifeline: the food a neighbor brings to the door, a peaceful sit in a lilac-filled park, a gentle touch of understanding, a homemade card of a child. Needing all the emotional help we can get, we notice all those small things that sustain us while we wait.

British author and spiritual director Margaret Silf tells of visiting a dying friend and his wife over a period of nine months. She recalls being lifted and inspired by this couple's attention to small things:

> My friend would invariably say, "Let's tell Margaret about the things that have been really good during this week." And I would sit and listen as they recounted a story of someone who had visited and brought them a piece of news or a new insight or perspective on the world, or maybe one of them had been reading something that moved him or her.
>
> Nearly every week I left with a book they had lent me or a poem or an article they had photocopied for me to read. Perhaps they would have received a letter. Or maybe a new flower had come out in the garden. Or they had spotted a visiting bird. Often the good thing of that week was a flash of memory that one of them had experienced or a dream that had left them feeling calm or at peace or simply an act of kindness—a neighbor had called, a son or daughter had phoned, the nurse had been gentle, the mailman had told a joke. . . .[6]

For thirteen years I have been attending and sometimes leading a women's spirituality program at my church called "Sisterspace." I look forward to gathering with friends and talking about the joys and struggles of our lives. Over the years, it has become a tradition at Sisterspace to go around the circle and share what we have come to call our "Miracles." This periodic review offers all of us a chance to ask ourselves, "What were the large or small events in my life during the past few weeks that seemed truly miraculous to me?" Sometimes people's answers are big and dramatic: a loved one's life has been saved or medical tests have come back blessedly negative for the presence of disease. But at other times answers are small and, at first hearing, almost insignificant: a crocus is blooming on the front step after an interminably long winter, or the finch is building her nest once again in the same place above the garage. Most of all, this time of sharing miracles has taught each of us to look at life through the lens of gratitude, appreciating the small things, taking nothing for granted.

Waiting offers us a unique time to make a home in our hearts for gratitude. As with any spiritual discipline, however, gratitude takes practice. Here are some practices that have helped me learn to live as a grateful person:

- List your sources of abundance (your health, your family, your training and experience, your home, etc.)[7]
- Think over the past year. Make a list of your answered prayers.
- Ask this question every night: For what do I give thanks today?
- Practice *finding* instead of *seeking.*[8]

We seem obsessed with more and more, continually seeking: seeking more knowledge, seeking a larger stockpile of material things, seeking a greater accumulation of exotic and stimulating experiences. Let your times of waiting help you take a little rest from constant and wearisome seeking. Think of the book title of the quote at the beginning of this section: *How to Want What You Have.* Reflect on the meaning of those words. Let waiting help you reflect with gratitude on what you have.

Spiritual Practice: An Old-Fashioned Prayer of Thanks

I thank Thee, God, that I have lived
In this great world and known its many joys;
The song of the birds, the strong, sweet scent of hay
And cooling breezes in the secret dusk,
The flaming sunsets at the close of day,
Hills, and the lonely, heather-covered moors,
Music at night, and moonlight on the sea,
The beat of waves upon the rocky shore

And, wild, white spray, flung high in ecstasy:
The faithful eyes of dogs, and treasured books.
The love of kin and fellowship of friends,
And all that makes life dear and beautiful.
I thank Thee, too, that there has come to me
A little sorrow and, sometimes, defeat,
A little heartache and the loneliness
That comes with parting, and the word, "Goodbye,"
Dawn breaking after dreary hours of pain,
When I discovered that night's gloom must yield
And morning light break through to me again.
Because of these and other blessings poured
Unasked upon my wondering head,
Because I know that there is yet to come
An even richer and more glorious life,
And most of all, because Thine only Son
Once sacrificed life's loveliness for me—
I thank Thee, God, that I have lived.[9]
  —Elizabeth, Countess of Craven, England (1750-1828)

Reflect on this prayer of thanksgiving. Think about all that you hold precious. Write your own prayer of thanksgiving.

Questions to Ponder
Gratitude turns obstacles into opportunity.
• Christina Baldwin says, "Life is a great unending opportunity to see things differently, to keep reframing disaster and discouragement into faith."[10] What could you reframe in your life right now? What difference could this make?
• What are you learning and how are you growing from having to wait?

Gratitude moves us beyond entitlement.
• What kinds of circumstances tend to make you feel entitled? How does this interfere with gratitude?

- The next time you are waiting—in line, on the phone, in traffic—take a very deep breath. Let yourself breathe in gratitude for one thing. Then make one very large exhale, breathing out entitlement.

Gratitude opens our eyes to the blessings of small things.
- Think of a time of waiting when you were comforted by small things. Make a list of the things you remember.
- Be on the alert in the coming week to periods of waiting. The next time you have to wait, use the opportunity to be grateful for one small thing.
- There are many ways to practice gratitude. What has already worked for you? What ideas from this chapter would you like to try?

The Sixth Gift of Waiting:
Humility

Sometimes we wait because we can't do anything else. We recognize that we are powerless. That powerlessness can be a spiritual opening. In our vulnerability, we realize that forces and powers far greater than ourselves have taken over. It is during those times of waiting that we learn humility.

Have you ever sat at the bedside of a loved one who was dying? Waiting is inevitable. It is a time of realizing you can't fix anything. You can't change anything. All you can do is quiet down and be a faithful presence. Waiting then becomes a holy and sanctified act. Waiting becomes grace-filled.

> *While boasting may be the opposite of humility, true humility is not the result of self-deprecation. It is, rather, the fruit of a keen-eyed ability to see oneself realistically, as a flawed and gifted creature like all other human beings. . . .*[1]
> —Robert C. Morris, "Meek as Moses"

HUMILITY LEADS US TO THE GRACE OF GOD.

Two springs ago our daughter, Kate, stayed on campus for a friend's baccalaureate service and graduation. The baccalaureate speaker at Kenyon College that year was Professor Perry Lentz. This celebrated professor of English and American Literature, this teacher to generations of Kenyon students, and this author of two famous civil war novels, stood up and said, "My name is Perry, and I am an alcoholic." Kate told us that his story was fresh, miraculous—yet so painful that he could not bring himself to make eye contact with his audience. He kept his head down as he recounted his forty years of drinking and his thirty-year saga of trying to hide his dependence on alcohol. He confessed to the graduating students that he usually took his first drink of the day right after the end of his 8:00 A.M. class, that he was "obsessed with securing alcohol and hated living a life of lies and deceptions."

On that May afternoon, Professor Lentz admitted this speech was "about the hardest thing I've ever done." Yet he saw it as an opportunity to come clean with anyone whom he had treated badly in the throes of his disease, an attempt to apologize to those who had seen him stumbling drunk on public occasions at the college. He told his audience that he was no longer living a lie, that he was more spiritually free than he had been in years. He talked at length about the overwhelming power of grace. He said he never could have gotten sober without admitting his powerlessness before God. "My change seems to be a miracle of grace."

Professor Lentz received a standing ovation from the four hundred graduating students, their families, and friends, many of whom were groping for tissues. My daughter will remember this speech and its profound lessons as long as she lives.

Stretched by humility, supported by the openness, generosity, and compassion of his colleagues and students, strengthened by the grace of a Higher Power, Professor Lentz had discovered the core meaning of the Apostle Paul's statement in Philippians 4:13: "I can do all things through [the one] who strengthens me."

We all feel powerless over something in our lives—maybe especially waiting. Our first instinct may be to rail against the powerlessness, to try to *do* something about it. Powerlessness is not something we welcome, and we might do everything we can to avoid it. But when we can let the powerlessness of waiting lead us to humility, to admitting that we are not in charge, we can move into a place where we can lean on God. And when we lean on God, we receive grace—grace that changes everything. God's grace provides relief and restoration and invites us to embrace outcomes we would never have believed possible.

HUMILITY LEADS US TO LOVE RATHER THAN ACHIEVEMENT.

When I was in seminary, I was fortunate to have Henri Nouwen as my spirituality professor. After I graduated, I continued to keep track of Henri, what country he was in, on which university faculty he served. After teaching in one Ivy league school after another, and after producing a book a year, Henri found himself disillusioned, burned out, and looking for deeper meaning. For the last eight years of his life, excluding his sabbatical year, he served as the pastor at Daybreak, a L'Arche community for the mentally and physically disabled near Toronto, Canada. He had finally found home in this place, where the residents had no idea that he was famous and that he had written dozens of books. They loved him because of who he was, not for what he had achieved.

When Henri moved to Daybreak, in addition to serving as pastor, he took on the personal responsibility of caring for Adam, a young man in his twenties who was severely disabled, a young man who could not walk, talk, feed, or dress himself. Until Adam's death eight years later, Henri spent two hours each morning and two hours each evening getting Adam up and putting Adam to bed.

On one occasion, Henri received an invitation to come to the Clinton White House. Hillary Clinton had been reading his books, had become intrigued by his writings on gratitude and forgiveness, and wanted his counsel. Henri declined. He later told a friend, "I don't want to be the court chaplain. I am here with Adam, my disabled friend. There are others who can go to the White House. Adam needs me."[2]

Waiting—especially long-term waiting—can give us a similar perspective. When we are not so busy *doing*, we have a chance to recognize who we *are*. When waiting puts life as we know it on hold, it is often a time when priorities get rearranged. We may reevaluate what is important and what is not. The things that we pushed so hard for, or worked so long for, may pale in the exposure of waiting. The things that we so proudly achieved may recede into the background.

These moments of humble awareness that love is more lasting than achievement may be some of the most valuable gifts of waiting.

HUMILITY LEADS US TO HONOR OTHERS.

Do you remember the line from the old Shaker song "Simple Gifts": *When true simplicity is gained, to bow and to bend we will not be ashamed?* I want to talk a little about bowing. The insightful psychologist and Buddhist monk Jack Kornfield talks of learning to bow as part of his spiritual practice. He recalls his experience at a monastery in Thailand where he began his training. He was told by a senior monk that he was expected to bow to his elders:

> So I began to bow to them. Sometimes it was just fine—there were quite a few wise and worthy elders in the community. But sometimes it felt ridiculous. I would encounter some twenty-one-year-old monk, full of hubris, who was there only to please his parents or to eat better food than he could at home, and I had to bow because he had been ordained the week before me. Or I had to bow to a sloppy old rice farmer who had come to the monastery the season before on the farmers' retirement plan, who chewed betel nut constantly

and had never meditated a day in his life. It was hard to pay reverence to these fellow forest dwellers as if they were great masters.[3]

Kornfield discovered, however, that he eventually began to enjoy bowing, that after a while, this spiritual practice created a certain open-heartedness and attentiveness to each person:

> Finally, as I prepared yet again for a day of bowing to my "elders," I began to look for some worthy aspect in each person I bowed to. I bowed to the wrinkles around the retired farmer's eyes, for all the difficulties he had seen and suffered through and triumphed over. I bowed to the vitality and playfulness in the young monks, the incredible possibilities each of their lives held yet ahead of them.[4]

When our family has traveled to India, one of my favorite parts of the trip is the bowing. Even though I am not fluent in Hindi as is my husband, I can put my hands together at my heart, say *"Namaste,"* and bow. With just one word and a simple bow, I can convey deep respect. I have always loved this ritual, this tender greeting that acknowledges the essence and gifts of another. It is one way of saying, "The divine in me greets the divine in thee."

Sometimes the despair of waiting can bring us low. One of the hidden gifts in this position is a change in perspective. From our low point, we can become aware of those around us who are struggling, who face their own waiting and despair. Think of it as a chance to bow to each other, to recognize our common humanity. Look at the worth of each individual. Respect the courage with which each person is facing his or her struggle. Honor—in yourself and in those who wait with and around you—the incredible value of the human journey.

HUMILITY LEADS US TO LIVE WITHOUT JUDGMENT.

Last summer I had trouble with my right leg, and my ortho-pedic surgeon told me to go shoe shopping. "The shoes I am recommending are going to cost you," he said, "but they will fit you perfectly." After I finally pumped out of him that the shoes were going to cost over one hundred dollars, I was determined to make sure mine were going to fit me perfectly! I walked into the shoe store and was crestfallen when a very young-looking girl walked up and asked if she could help. Arrogantly, I said, "I need a person who knows a great deal about shoes. Are you that person?"

I fully expected her to say, "No, but I can find somebody." Instead, she said, "I think I can help you." In a huff, I sat down and consented to be helped.

Not swayed by my critical demeanor, this young person pro-ceeded to do her job well, to fit the right shoe to my foot with kindness and competence. Because she was such a professional, the shoe fitting took a full twenty minutes, and eventually I found myself in conversation. When I asked if she were in school, she told me she had graduated from college and was presently at Marquette University completing the second year of a three-year doctorate in physical therapy. Chagrined to discover her true chronological age, as well as her degree of knowledge, I had to admit that she knew a great deal about shoes and feet. It was cer-tainly a lesson for me in not judging other people.

Have you ever had the experience of getting impatient while you are waiting, and deeming the person who is supposed to be helping you incompetent? You may feel critical; you may think someone higher up the ladder—someone more skilled, someone more experienced, someone in charge—could get or fix or imple-ment what you've been waiting for. While this may be accurate at times, eagerness to get the best may blind us to the very help that is available to us. The next time you feel impatient about waiting, see if waiting has a small lesson to teach you in humility. Take a look around: Who is trying to help you? How can you respect what they have to offer? What is their perspective on this? What can you receive from them?

Humility leads us to honest assessment.

Humility is a curious animal. I have had a love/hate relationship with it for years. Many of the people I see on retreats and in spiritual direction don't need humility. They've been beaten down enough. They have been told time after time that they are worthless or inadequate. Most of us have little trouble naming our flaws and our failures. Many of us have a far more difficult time living into our giftedness. We often refuse to accept our belovedness, and occasionally, we throw back in God's face the unique and amazing talents we have been given. Yes, we need to consider our sins and our failings, but we also need to lift up our gifts and honor our God-given talents.

The word *humility* is from the Latin word *humus*, which means ground or earth. True humility grounds us in understanding who we really are, the whole truth of it, both positive and negative. The author of the fourteenth-century classic *The Cloud of Unknowing* instructs us to "strain every nerve in every possible way to know and experience yourself [accurately] as you really are."[5] Benedictine prioress Joan Chittister says, "Humility is the ability to know ourselves as God knows us."[6] First Samuel 16:7b says "GOD sees not as people see; people look on the outward appearance, but GOD looks on the heart."[7] Methodist pastor and writer Keith Beasley-Topliffe says, "Humble abandonment does not only mean being brought low. It means accepting whatever task God assigns us. That can even mean being exulted."[8]

In essence, these writers are all conveying the same message: Humility means authentically assessing our gifts and our potential as much as our failings and sins. True humility requires accepting our goodness as well as our flaws.

Hear these startling and empowering words from Marianne Williamson:

Our deepest fear
>is not that we are inadequate.
Our deepest fear
>is that we are powerful beyond measure.
It is our light,
>not our darkness,
>>that most frightens us.
We ask ourselves,
>who am I to be brilliant,
>>gorgeous, talented, fabulous?

Actually, who are you *not* to be?

You are a child of God.

Your playing small
>doesn't serve the world.
There's nothing enlightened about shrinking
>so that other people
>>won't feel insecure around you.

We were born to make manifest
>the glory of God that is within us.
It's not just in some of us;
>it's in everyone.
And as we let our own light shine,
>we unconsciously give other people
>>permission to do the same.
As we are liberated from our own fear,
>our presence automatically liberates others.[9]

There may be no more provoking experience than being told, "Wait." It stops any action we might take. We may feel powerless, unprotected. Someone else holds all the cards. In the intervening moments—or days or weeks or years—waiting beckons us to come to the well of humility, to drink deeply. Those clarifying waters give us a chance to see ourselves clearly: to see both our flaws and our gifts, to accept both our failings and our goodness.

Even the waiting itself becomes a lens through which we can assess ourselves honestly. The next time you find yourself waiting, consider your response. How much do you assert yourself to get things done, to end the waiting? Acknowledge your confidence, your decisiveness. How much do you seek advice and support? Acknowledge your ability to listen and discern.

Then give thanks, in humility, that you are a child of God "born to make manifest the glory of God."

Spiritual Practice: A Daily Inventory

For one week, before you go to sleep each night, ask yourself the following two questions:

> *On shortcomings:* For what actions today do I need to repent?
> *On giftedness:* How have I used my God-given gifts today?

Questions to Ponder

Humility leads us to the grace of God.

- Think of a time when you had to wait for something and felt powerless. Did you have any sense of needing to rely on a power greater than yourself? How did you pray?
- Name an occasion during the past week when you were conscious of God's grace. Include this in a prayer of thanksgiving.

Humility leads us to love rather than achievement.

- Have you ever had an experience of waiting where you had to reevaluate what was important? What was the result?
- Does a drivenness to achieve ever get in your way?
- How might you live more comfortably out of love rather than achievement?

Humility leads us to honor others.
- Think of a time in your life when waiting helped you recognize your common humanity. How did this give you a sense of respect for others who waited?
- Think of one way you might honor someone today.
- Think of someone whom you are having trouble honoring. How might you pray about this?

Humility leads us to live without judgment.
- How quick are you to judge people? On a scale from 1 to 10, with 1 being the slowest and 10 being the fastest, where would you place yourself?
- Use your times of waiting this week to practice being nonjudgmental. Make note of who is helping you while you wait. Thank them for their efforts.

Humility leads us to honest assessment.
- In the week ahead, use any time that you have to wait as a time for a mini-assessment. How are you responding to the wait? What good qualities come out? What emerges that bothers you?
- Is there a flawed or struggling part of yourself that you're having difficulty with? Bring it to God in prayer.
- Is there a good or gifted part of you that you are hesitant to acknowledge? Bring this to your prayer as well.

The Seventh Gift of Waiting:

Trust in God

When we can't control things and when we can't predict the future, we begin to live in trust.

How many cancer survivors do you know who actually talk about their disease with gratitude? Some of them speak appreciatively of their illness because it rearranged their lives. Because it taught them the richness of not knowing. Because it instilled in them the ability to trust. Survivors who have waited out the course of a disease know firsthand what it means to loosen their grasp and to develop trust in God.

This may well be the greatest gift of waiting. Trust in God takes us beyond self-reliance into new depths of faith. Trust in God invites us to let go of our fears, to open our hearts in prayer, and to trust in the boundless love and care that God has for us.

Eficacia De La Paciencia	*"Efficacy of Patience"*
Nada te turbe,	*Let nothing trouble you,*
Nada te espante,	*Let nothing scare you,*
Todo se pasa,	*All is fleeting,*
Dios no se muda,	*God alone is unchanging.*
La Paciencia	*Patience*
Todo lo alcanza;	*Everything obtains.*
Quien a Dios tiene	*Who possesses God*
Nada le falta.	*Nothing wants.*
Sólo Dios basta.	*God alone suffices.* [1]

—Teresa of Avila (1515-1582)

TRUST IN GOD IS AN INVITATION TO LET GO OF FEAR.

You who live in the shelter of the Most High,
who abide in the shadow of the Almighty,
will say to GOD, "My refuge and my fortress;
my God, in whom I trust." [2]
   —Psalm 91:1-2

The most challenging part of pregnancy is the watching and waiting to see what happens without being able to do a thing about it. Once pregnancy gets started, a new life begins, and the mother is part of a creative process that is way beyond her control. She cannot regulate this astonishing growth. She gets bigger and bigger and bigger. The baby kicks harder and harder and harder. The pregnant woman needs to trust that things will turn out all right, or that she will have the strength, with God's help, to manage if they do not. It is a potently frightening and spiritually challenging time. A mother-to-be learns quickly what trust in God is all about.

When I was two weeks away from giving birth to my first child, I spent a great deal of time wondering how I would know if labor had definitively started, how I would get to the hospital, and what kind of anesthesia I might or might not need. I also spent time reading the birth narratives in the Gospels, and the word of God hit me directly in my very pregnant abdomen. My concerns seemed rather trivial and self-indulgent when compared to Mary's wearying ninety-mile journey from Nazareth to Bethlehem on foot and on donkey. But it was not the *physical* stamina of Mary that caused me to marvel most; it was her *spiritual* stamina, her absolute trusting faith in God in the face of bewildering circumstances.

It is hard enough for any mother worrying about delivery complications or possible birth defects, without having some angel drop in and tell you that you have been chosen to bear the Son of God. I am awestruck by Mary's trust. That winter of my first pregnancy, I realized that even a so-called normal, non-divine pregnancy demands a great deal of trust, let alone a pregnancy in the astonishing circumstances in which Mary found herself. Here she was, a teenager, scared, confused, socially ostracized, who nevertheless managed to say, "Let it be with me according to your word" (Luke 1:38).

"Let it be with me according to your word." Mary trusted God enough to make herself available to God in this extraordinary way.

In her poem "Annunciation," Denise Levertov writes of Mary:

> She did not cry, "I cannot, I am not worthy,"
> nor, "I have not the strength."
> She did not submit with gritted teeth,
> > raging, coerced.
> Bravest of all humans,
> > consent illumined her.
> The room filled with its light,
> the lily glowed in it,
> > and the iridescent wings.
> Consent,
> > courage unparalleled,
> opened her utterly.[3]

✓Waiting opens us to vulnerability and fear, but also to strength ✓and courage. Waiting always gives us an opportunity to trust that God is at work in our particular situation.

It has been said that "Pregnancy is a receiving partnership in grace."[4] We are all—men and women—called upon to be "pregnant" at times, to enter a period of waiting for growth and new life. Like Mary, we, too, are called by God to say, "Let it be with me according to your word." Our waiting holds the potential for new life—and the invitation to trust God.

Have you ever felt afraid to act? Or afraid that the choice you made might be wrong? Afraid that the new life you've begun—by moving to a new community, or adopting a child, or going back to school, or taking a new job, or retiring—will not work out as you had hoped?

Sometimes in my work in spiritual direction, when a person is doubting God's involvement in circumstances, I will ask them to go home and find a container (a Mason jar or a bowl or a box) to represent God's In Box.[5] I ask them to write down their concerns and drop them in. God's In Box becomes a visual representation of God's care and keeping. They can look at the container and be reminded that they are not alone, that God "will neither slumber nor sleep" (Psalm 121:4b), and that God is holding their concern. This ritual is a reminder that God has been at work and will be at work in their lives, that God takes their worries seriously.

The next time you are waiting, picture placing your fears in the box. Let the waiting lead you to trust, and let your trust in God lead you beyond your fears.

TRUST IN GOD IS AN INVITATION TO TRUST IN LOVE.

When we find ourselves waiting for something major to happen in our lives, we may console ourselves with the thought, "God's will be done." Yet that phrase often conjures up dour faces and tragic voices entoning such statements as, "It must have been God's will that she was taken so young," or "It must have been God's will that he didn't live to witness his father's suicide." We rarely hear, "It must have been God's will that I had gratifying and loving sex" or "It must have been God's will that I got the promotion at work." Is it any wonder that we have trouble trusting?

Waiting gives us an opportunity to practice trusting God as the One "who richly provides us with everything for our enjoyment" (1 Timothy 6:17b). Why do we hang on to the notion that God's will for us is grief or suffering? Why do we believe that after a period of good fortune or much happiness "the other shoe is going to drop" or God is going to zap us? It just might be God's will that we experience deep joy or profound resurrection.

Hear these words of Thomas Merton:

> If we do not pray, it is because we sometimes hold superstitions, one form being this: if I give myself up too much to God, God will give me something too hard which I cannot do. This is not Christian maturity. It presupposes that Our Lord is playing tricks with us all the time. We have to get rid of the thought that God is a powerful deceiver, that God is ready to catch us in some moment of weakness and impose some terrible punishment. This is a dreadful concept of God. The first thing is to root out every vestige of this thought of God. Don't think God is trying to catch you. . . .
>
> Open yourself to God. God will never, never fail us. We have to really believe we are totally forgiven. Don't set limits to the mercy of God. . . .[6]

Many of us need practice in understanding that God's will for us is life-giving and positive, that God is on our side. The next time you are waiting for something important, think of it as a built-in opportunity to put flesh and bones on your trust, to put words into practice—and to experience the blessings of God's mercy. Minister and counselor Wayne Muller suggests that when we think of the words, "Thy will be done," we substitute the words, "Thy love be done."[7] Try it out for yourself. See how

"Thy love be done" changes your level of trust—and the quality of your waiting.

Trust God to lead you to far greater things than you could have ever imagined.

TRUST IN GOD IS AN INVITATION TO PRAY.

> Unsleeping friend,
> when I come to the end of my strength,
> and my work has no blessing in it,
> help me to remember you,
> to reach for the hand of a friend
> and find your love is here.[8]
> —Bernard Thorogood, Australia

While we wait, life can sometimes be overwhelming. Sometimes our options seem so complicated or confusing that we don't even know what we want, or we lose sight of exactly what we are waiting for. Waiting presents us with a choice: To give in to the quagmire, or to give the quagmire up to prayer.

A friend of mine told me that when he was in parochial school, the nuns would always say, "Offer it up. Offer it up." There's a lot of value in this. Waiting gives us a chance to "offer it up." Even— or especially—if we don't have the "right" words, or know how to pray, waiting stretches us beyond our normal, routine prayers.

What if we really believed the words of the Lord's Prayer: "Thy will be done?" Many of us pray that prayer each Sunday, but how often do we pause to ponder the radical implications of that prayer? "Thy will be done" means trusting implicitly that God is working alongside us for good. "Thy will be done" means trusting that God's judgment is wiser and deeper than our own. The beloved and familiar scripture from Romans 8:26 teaches us about God's abiding with us and reminds us that "we do not know how to pray as we ought, but [the] Spirit intercedes [for us] with sighs too deep for words."

I have learned a great deal from my Quaker friends about letting God decide. When they are asked to pray, they say simply, "I will hold you in the light." This prayer of absolute trust, which delights in God's awesome wisdom, sits in contrast to the highly controlled wish list of desired outcomes that many of us frequently present to God. This kind of prayer finds its peace in the plan God thinks best. It is a prayer of surrender to the larger picture of God's love.

While we are waiting, God is always waiting for us. Early Christianity scholar Roberta Bondi says, "We can be certain that God desires our friendship, and, indeed, created us for this end."[9] These touching words are true. God yearns to take part in a mutual relationship. God is waiting to listen to our prayers and is eager to show us love.

Waiting. We cannot escape it. We will be waiting all of our lives for one thing or another. There are little waits and big waits, gratifying waits and excruciating waits—and we can learn from all of them. As we practice these new spiritual lessons, our learning curve may be steep. Waiting immerses us in a different kind of time and bids us to pay attention, but waiting is a patient teacher and offers generous gifts: patience, loss of control, living in the present, compassion, gratitude, humility, and trust in God. Waiting teaches us to embrace our own resilience and courage, to believe that others will reach out to help, and to know that God's love will always find us.

Thanks be to God.

Spiritual Practice: Thy Will Be Done

> Creator, whatever it is you want me to do today,
> this is what I want to do.
>
> Whatever it is you want me to say, today, Creator,
> that is what I want to say.
>
> Wherever it is you want me to go today, Creator,
> that is where I want to go.[10]
>   —Sequoyah, a Native American

Practice praying this prayer each morning for a week. Pay attention to any changes you experience in your spiritual life.

Questions to Ponder
Trust in God is an invitation to let go of fear.
- If you are waiting for something important right now in your life, what fears do you have? If you are not in a waiting period right now, what is your experience of past fears you have struggled with?
- What might you do to let go of these fears? Where is God's invitation in this?

Trust in God is an invitation to trust in love.
- After a period of happiness and good fortune, are you afraid "the other shoe will drop"?
- How much do you trust that God loves you? How might you use a period of waiting to practice trusting that love?
- How does the phrase "Thy love be done" strike you? Where in your life might you use that phrase right now?

Trust in God is an invitation to pray.
- How do you pray these days? Is there anything you'd like to change about that?

- Is there any waiting in your life right now that you'd like to "offer up" to God?
- What lies between "my will be done" and "thy will be done?" Is that a scary place for you?
- How do you feel about the idea of God waiting for you?

How to Use This Book
with a Group

This book can be used for group study at any time during the year, but it is especially ideal for the weeks leading up to Christmas, before or during Advent, and during Lent.

Another option is to use the one-day retreat outlined at the close of the book for a group. It provides a good overview of the gifts of waiting. (Note: If you choose to do a weekly group, you will not want to use the retreat in addition, since it would be repetitive.)

If you are preparing to lead a group, as you read the chapters take notes on what seems particularly interesting or conducive to discussion. Pay special attention to the Spiritual Practice section of each chapter and think about how you might help participants reflect on this. Decide how you will make time for the Spiritual Practice with your group: either by dividing into small groups, or giving people space for solitude, or remaining in the large group for discussion.

Here are some suggestions to make your group experience beneficial:

1. Ask participants to read the appropriate chapters ahead of time in preparation for each group meeting.
2. Provide a kind and generous welcome.

3. Make sure you and each participant are adequately introduced. (You may want to use name tags.)

4. Say in your own words why this study is taking place and introduce the topic of waiting as a spiritual opportunity and a spiritual gift.

5. As you begin, ask each person to turn to page 18 and to read in unison the Scripture from Isaiah 40:28-31.

6. Write on newsprint the subheadings of the chapter(s) you will cover in each session (see the Contents.)

7. Ask the group what caught their attention in this chapter.

8. Use the Spiritual Practice and Questions to Ponder sections of each chapter to create group exercises and discussion. Vary the experience so that there is a balance of quiet time for thinking and writing, and both large and small group sharing.

9. As you move toward adjournment, remind the group when the next session will be and what chapter(s) they should read in preparation.

10. End each session with your own prayer or ask the participants to join you in this unison prayer:

> Gracious God of all times and places,
> We thank you that you are with
> our going out and our coming in,
> our stopping and our waiting.
> May waiting be our teacher.
> Bless us we pray. Amen

For a four-week study series, study two chapters each week:
    Session One: Introduction and Patience
    Session Two: Loss of Control and Living in the Present
    Session Three: Compassion and Gratitude
    Session Four: Humility and Trust in God

These sessions should be 1 1/2 to 2 hours in length. Work with one chapter at a time and take a stretch break between chapters.

For an eight-week study series, study one chapter each week:

Session One: Introduction

Session Two: Patience

Session Three: Loss of Control

Session Four: Living in the Present

Session Five: Compassion

Session Six: Gratitude

Session Seven: Humility

Session Eight: Trust in God

These sessions should be 45 minutes to 1 hour in length. For the first session, rather than assigning reading material ahead, use the time to present the content of the Introduction. Ask the group to discuss how waiting has accompanied various stages of their lives. Invite them to share how these periods of waiting have been teachers. You might want to give people time to meditate on the Rumi poem, to consider what kinds of waiting have visited their "guest house" over the years, and what they have learned.

Retreat:

A Spirituality of Waiting

THEME

This one-day retreat will help you understand the spiritual gifts of waiting, deepen your insights about waiting, and open you to receive the gifts that waiting holds for you.

Planning Ahead

During the week before your retreat, ask yourself these questions:

- How do I respond to waiting?
- What am I waiting for now?

Let your answers simmer as you go about your daily activities.

If you are doing this retreat with a group
LEADER: In addition to reflecting on these questions, become familiar with the seven gifts of waiting. Read the material from the introductions to each chapter (collected on page 101-105) for an overview of the gifts. Pray for yourself and each retreat participant.

Before your retreat day, collect the following materials, so you won't be distracted during your retreat:
- journal
- Bible
- some songs or hymns or selections of music to play
- small table on which to create an altar
- cloth to place over the table, and perhaps some flowers
- candle and lighter or matches
- clock
- three stones

If you are doing this retreat with a group
LEADER: Ask people to bring journals and Bibles. In addition to songs, music, and the materials suggested above for an altar, you will need:
- extra Bibles (to ensure that everyone will have one for the Bible study)
- three stones for each person
- an easel with newsprint
- a prayer of invocation for Centering

Prepare the following newsprint and handout sheets ahead of time:
- Write on newsprint the words to Psalm 130:5-6 (page 100).
- Prepare a handout sheet with the Morning Reflection journaling questions (pages 105-106).
- Write on newsprint the Prayer Before Eating (page 107), changing singular pronouns to plural.
- Write on newsprint the words to Isaiah 40:28-31 (page 108).
- Choose a passage for the Bible Study (page 109) and write the reference on

newsprint, along with the study guidelines for small groups (page 109).
- Select the excerpts you want to use for the Afternoon Reflection and write the corresponding reflection question for each on separate newsprint sheets (page 110).
- Write on newsprint the instructions for the Spiritual Practice (page 111).
- Write on newsprint the Blessing (page 113), changing singular pronouns to plural.

CREATING SACRED SPACE

Create an altar table with a decorative cloth, perhaps some flowers, a lighted candle, and a clock to represent the time of waiting. Add the three stones you have selected for this retreat.

If you are doing this retreat with a group
LEADER: As you prepare the altar, arrange the stones you have brought for the retreatants either on the altar or on the floor near the altar.

MORNING (about 2 to 2 1/4 hours)

WELCOME (allow about 5-10 minutes)

Welcome this new day. Stretch your arms toward the sky, inhaling deeply your hopes for the day, exhaling whatever anxieties you wish to put aside. After repeating this several times, sing or play a favorite piece of music to quiet your heart.

> *If you are doing this retreat with a group*
> LEADER: After leading the group in this stretch-
> ing, inhaling, and exhaling, welcome the group
> and describe the day's agenda. Suggest a song
> for the group to sing together or play a quieting
> piece of music.

CENTERING *(allow about 10-20 minutes)*

Sit for a few minutes in silence, breathing in and breathing out. Use the words "Be here now" as a mantra. When your thoughts drift, return to the phrase "Be here now."

Prayerfully ponder any distractions or obstacles that may be blocking you from receiving this retreat fully. Pass these over to God's loving care.

Next, sit for a few minutes in silence and offer a prayer of invocation asking God's blessing on your retreat.

Then affirm the theme of the day by speaking aloud the fifth and sixth verses of Psalm 130. Repeat the verses, the second time letting them sink in a little more deeply.

> I wait for GOD, my soul waits,
>   and in God's word I hope;
> my soul waits for GOD
>   more than those who watch for the morning,
>   more than those who watch for the morning.[1]

> *If you are doing this retreat with a group*
> LEADER: After directing the group in a time
> of centering with the phrase "Be here now,"
> and passing obstacles over to God's loving
> care, pray aloud a prayer of invocation, ask-
> ing God's blessing on the day. Display the

newsprint sheet of Psalm 130 and lead the group in reading those verses aloud two times. After this, allow some time for introductions. If the group is fewer than twenty, go around the circle briefly, answering the question: "What is the hardest thing for you about waiting?" If the group is larger, have people share their responses in small groups.

MEDITATION (*allow about 15 minutes*)

Read (or re-read) the following material collected from the introductions to each chapter in this book.

"Seven Spiritual Gifts of Waiting"

The Bible has many dramatic stories about waiting. The Israelites wandered in the wilderness for forty years waiting to get into the Promised Land. Jacob waited fourteen years before winning the hand of Rachel, his beloved. The Apostle Paul waited over and over to be released from prison. Jesus waited forty days in the desert tempted by the devil.

In her beloved hymn "Lead On, O Cloud of Yahweh," hymn writer Ruth Duck affirms:

We are not lost, though wandering,
     for by your light we come,
and we are still God's people.
     The journey is our home.[2]

"The journey is our home." And our journey will always include waiting. If we are going to continue to live, we are going to continue to wait. The good news is that the discipline of waiting offers us seven spiritual gifts:

The first gift of waiting is patience.
The second gift of waiting is loss of control.
The third gift of waiting is the living in the present.
The fourth gift of waiting is compassion.
The fifth gift of waiting is gratitude.
The sixth gift of waiting is humility.
The seventh gift of waiting is trust in God.

May the God who loves us help us all learn how to wait.

The First Gift of Waiting: PATIENCE
Waiting teaches us to live life in increments, in small pieces rather than large chunks. Waiting teaches us to measure our progress slowly. Alcoholics and addicts know this more than most of us: They measure their years of recovery in single days. They know that their waiting in recovery takes place one day at a time.

Psalm 25 talks specifically about waiting on God: "You are the God of my salvation; for you I wait all day long" (25:5). It is hard to wait on God. Whether we're freeing ourselves from addiction, healing from a long illness, adopting a baby, or waiting for word to come through about a job or a house or a school, it is hard to trust the slow unfolding of God's action. God's time is different from our time. In God's time, we are often waiting for the bigger picture but must be content with each small piece. When we are waiting, we put one foot in front of the other every morning and every evening. Waiting teaches us patience.

The Second Gift of Waiting: LOSS OF CONTROL
For those of us for whom staying in control is the ultimate achievement, loss of control seems like a perverse and rotten gift indeed. The release of control, though, can be an empowering spiritual step.

Not long ago, coming back from the East Coast, I was unexpectedly caught in severe weather. As we departed, the skies looked fine, but the situation changed dramatically an hour-and-a-half later. It was then that the pilot announced, "We're circling Milwaukee, which is presently experiencing extremely severe weather." A half hour later the pilot declared, "It is still too dangerous to land in Milwaukee, and we are running low on fuel. We'll have to go to an alternate city to land." By this time, it was clear that everything was out of control. Connecting flights became impossible. It was uncertain whether we'd even be able to get into Milwaukee that same day.

At that point, we all gave up. When we accepted that everything was in pandemonium, life got easier. As we sat on the tarmac in Michigan, people spoke kindly to one another and passed their cell phones back and forth so everyone could call home. People began telling stories of where they were headed, of their families and jobs. We became more than silent strangers. We surrendered to forces beyond our control . . . and found each other.

The Third Gift of Waiting: LIVING IN THE PRESENT

Waiting teaches us to dwell fully where we are. When we can't control our circumstances and we can't predict the future, we have the opportunity to live in the present.

Sometimes after a huge Milwaukee blizzard, while we're waiting for the roads to be shoveled, we hear the news that schools will be closed and that everyone who can should stay home and off the highways. What a gift this news is! I can cancel my hard-nosed plans. I can go back to bed. I can write a few checks I meant to get to yesterday. I can make cookies with the kids. I can watch the movie from the video store that I rented three days ago. I can live in the present moment.

The Fourth Gift of Waiting: COMPASSION

When we are waiting for something important in our lives, we tend to seek out others who will understand our restlessness and anxieties. Think of the Advent story of Mary and her cousin Elizabeth, one young woman and one much older woman, both pregnant. They were both living in circumstances beyond their control, expecting an unexpected child, and in their fear and excitement they reached out to one another. Their shared waiting gave them a unique understanding of what each was going through, and they could embrace each other in compassion.

We, too, know the feeling of waiting with others, in uncertainty, in crisis. Maybe you've had the experience of waiting in the family members' lounge of the hospital intensive care unit. If so, you know the feeling of desperation and intense anxiety. You know the feeling of talking to a stranger sitting next to you and asking that person who their loved one is and what they are waiting for. You know the feeling of a stranger coming up to you and saying, "I'm going down to the cafeteria. Do you want to come? Can I bring you something back?" Even with total strangers, sharing fears and insecurities while we wait offers a bridge of understanding.

Waiting together in uncertainty creates compassion.

The Fifth Gift of Waiting: GRATITUDE
I hate waiting in line at the grocery store—but sometimes I see my full cart and am grateful I can afford this food. When I think of the people whom this food will feed, I am grateful for my family and the companionship at our table.

Waiting can give us unexpected moments to be grateful for everything that is peaceful or lovely or running smoothly, the small things we may not have noticed before. Waiting can inspire us to look around carefully and to observe what's there. Yes, we are waiting. But look at all these people who are offering help. Yes, we are waiting. But aren't we lucky we're going through this now rather than ten years ago?

Waiting teaches us to appreciate those pieces of our lives that have gracefully fallen into place. Waiting teaches us gratitude.

The Sixth Gift of Waiting: HUMILITY
Sometimes we wait because we can't do anything else. We recognize that we are powerless. That powerlessness can be a spiritual

opening. In our vulnerability, we can realize that forces and powers far greater than ourselves have taken over. It is during those times of waiting that we learn humility.

Have you ever sat at the bedside of a loved one who was dying? Waiting is inevitable. It is a time of realizing you can't fix anything. You can't change anything. All you can do is quiet down and be a faithful presence. Waiting then becomes a holy and sanctified act. Waiting becomes grace-filled.

The Seventh Gift of Waiting: TRUST IN GOD

When we can't control things and when we can't predict the future, we begin to live in trust.

How many cancer survivors do you know who actually talk about their disease with gratitude? Some of them speak appreciatively of their illness because it rearranged their lives. Because it taught them the richness of not knowing. Because it instilled in them the ability to trust. Survivors who have waited out the course of a disease know firsthand what it means to loosen their grasp and to develop trust in God.

This may well be the greatest gift of waiting. Trust in God takes us beyond self-reliance into new depths of faith. Trust in God invites us to let go of our fears, to open our hearts in prayer, and to trust in the boundless love and care that God has for us.

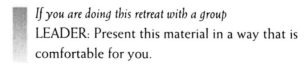

If you are doing this retreat with a group
LEADER: Present this material in a way that is comfortable for you.

MORNING REFLECTION *(allow about 1 1/2 hours)*

Play a quieting piece of music. Take your journal and settle into a comfortable place where you can reflect on these questions and record your thoughts and feelings:

- What has been your most potent experience of waiting?
- What did you learn about yourself?

- What are you waiting for now?
- Waiting offers a treasure chest of spiritual gifts. Select from the following questions those that speak to your current circumstances:

PATIENCE: Waiting teaches us to live life in small increments. What is your current waiting teaching you about this?

LOSS OF CONTROL: Waiting offers us a chance to let go. What might you let go of in your current waiting?

LIVING IN THE PRESENT: Waiting teaches us to dwell fully where we are. What can you find to appreciate in the "now" while you are waiting?

COMPASSION: Waiting offers us many opportunities for compassion—both to give and to receive. How are you experiencing compassion as you wait?

GRATITUDE: Waiting teaches us to value the small things. Ponder what you can be grateful for in your present circumstances.

HUMILITY: Waiting is a spiritual opening to recognize our powerlessness—and God's grace. What is your current waiting teaching you about humility?

TRUST IN GOD: Waiting teaches us to live in trust. How could you use your waiting to practice trusting God's love?

If you are doing this retreat with a group
LEADER: Give people the handout sheet you've prepared with the journaling questions. Direct them to take their journals to a place of solitude where they can quietly respond to the questions. Let them know they will have one

hour, and they can sit, walk, or go outside, as long as all can reflect in silence. After an hour, gather everyone back. Regroup by singing or stretching or listening to music. Then divide people into groups of four, counting off by the letters W-A-I-T (adjust for uneven groups as necessary.) Invite them to discuss the question "What are you waiting for now?" in their small groups for 15 minutes. Then ask every person to choose two gifts of waiting that speak most to them and share their thoughts in the small group. Allow about 15 more minutes for this. Signal with a small chime or bell, or some other nonintrusive sound, when it is time to move on.

A Prayer Before Eating

Gracious God of all times and places,
I thank you that you are with my going out
and my coming in,
my stopping, and my waiting.
Bless me and this food I pray. Amen

If you are doing this retreat with a group
LEADER: Display the newsprint sheet with the Prayer Before Eating. Ask the group to stand in a circle and hold hands while saying the prayer.

LUNCH AND FREE TIME (about 1 1/2 to 2 hours)

Optional question to ponder during free time:
• What is my waiting offering me?

If possible, walk outside, absorb the season, notice nature. If you can't go outside, consider relaxing with a new symbol or a new posture in front of a lighted candle.

AFTERNOON (about 2 to 2 1/4 hours)

CENTERING (allow about 15 minutes)
First, sing a song.

Then sit for a few minutes in silence, breathing in and breathing out. Use the words "God is near" as a mantra. When your thoughts drift, return to the phrase "God is near."

Finally, read aloud Isaiah 40:28-31.

> Have you not known? Have you not heard?
> The LORD is the everlasting God,
> the Creator of the ends of the earth.
> [God] does not faint or grow weary;
> [God's] understanding is unsearchable.
> [God] gives power to the faint,
> and strengthens the powerless.
> Even youths will faint and be weary,
> and the young will fall exhausted;
> but those who wait for the LORD
> shall renew their strength,
> they shall mount up with wings like eagles,
> they shall run and not be weary,
> they shall walk and not faint.

If you are doing this retreat with a group
LEADER: After leading the group in singing and centering, display the newsprint sheet with the Isaiah passage. Invite everyone to read the words in unison.

BIBLE STUDY (*allow about 20 minutes*)
Choose one of the following Scripture passages to read:

- for an Advent retreat: Luke 1:26-56
- for a Lenten retreat: Luke 4:1-12 or Luke 22:39-46
- for other times of the year: Psalm 37 or Psalm 62

Use your journal to record your thoughts and feelings about what you have read. Then consider these questions:

- What does the Scripture teach me about waiting?
- How does the Scripture inspire me to act?

If you are doing this retreat with a group
LEADER: Display the newsprint sheet with the reference you have selected for the Bible Study, along with the guidelines. Divide the larger group into smaller groups. Be sure everyone in the group has a Bible. Refer to the newsprint for these study guidelines:

- Have someone read the passage aloud slowly.
- Sit in silence for about 3 minutes, meditating on the passage.
- What does this Scripture teach you about waiting?
- How does this Scripture inspire you to act in your own life?

Ask each group to spend about 20 minutes following the study guidelines. At the end of the time, call the larger group back together.

INTERLUDE *(allow about 10 minutes)*
Pause to stretch or sing a song.

AFTERNOON REFLECTION *(allow about 45 minutes to 1 hour)*
Spend some time with some or all of the following excerpts from the book:

- Read the poem "What to Do in the Darkness" by Marilyn Chandler McEntyre on page 38. How do her words about practicing trust and watching for the dawn speak to your experience of waiting?
- Read the quotation from Etty Hillesum on page 43. How does her journal entry about being "sufficient unto the day" speak to your experience of trying to live in the present?
- Read the quotation from Eckhart Tolle on page 47. How do his words about people who are "waiting to start living" speak to your life?
- Read Lydia's story on page 51. What people make up your "cloud of witnesses" and assure you of their love?
- Read Margaret Silf's story of her dying friend and his wife on page 68. What does their attention to "small things" teach you about being grateful for the small things in your life?
- Read Marianne Williamson's piece on page 80. How does her reminder that "you are a child of God" empower you?

If you are doing this retreat with a group
LEADER: Select some or all of these excerpts to read aloud (either you can read the quotations or ask various volunteers to read them). After each excerpt, display the newsprint sheet

you have prepared with the appropriate reflection question. Invite participants to talk about whatever they are comfortable sharing. (You may also wish to give people time after each reading to write in their journals.)

(Take a brief stretch break if needed)

SPIRITUAL PRACTICE *(allow about 20 minutes)*
Pick up from the altar the three stones that you have selected for this retreat.

Give each stone the name of one gift of waiting that you would like to receive.

Take these stones in your hands and pray for God's blessing on your path of waiting.

If you are doing this retreat with a group
LEADER: Display the newsprint sheet with the instructions for this Spiritual Practice. Have each person get three stones from the altar. Give every person about 10 minutes to work with the stones and to pray in silence for God's blessing. Then ask if anyone in the group feels comfortable sharing the names of his or her stones aloud. Allow about 10 minutes for this sharing.

CLOSING RITUAL *(allow about 10 minutes)*
Read aloud this psalm.

"For Reassurance"

I shall wait in Your sight:
Prepare me with Your teachings;
Place knowledge as a screen,
A shelter against winds of adversity.

I shall wait in Your sight:
Animate me with Your teachings;
Invigorate my days with purpose,
Enlarge my actions with meaning.

I shall wait in Your sight:
Empower me with Your teachings;
Let my thirst never be quenched,
Let me drink from Your well.

I shall wait in Your sight.
Secure in who I am,
I will push back the webs of worry,
To face my daily challenges.

I shall wait in Your sight,
Secure in Who You are,
I will lean against Your teachings
To guide my daily acts.[3]
  —Debbie Perlman

BLESSING

Stand, as you are able, and cross your arms over your chest. Bless yourself with the words: "May God bless me in my waiting and in my trusting."

Close your retreat with quiet music or a song.

If you are doing this retreat with a group
LEADER: After reading the psalm "For Reassurance," display the newsprint sheet with the Blessing. Ask those who are able to stand in a circle, crossing their arms over their chests. Have the group read the Blessing in unison. End the retreat with a song.

Notes

Introduction

1. Anecdote from Margaret Guenther at the "Becoming a Bethlehem" retreat, Dekoven Retreat Center, Racine, Wisconsin, November 17-19, 2000. The author acknowledges her inspiration from Margaret's retreat for this introduction on waiting.

2. Jalal al-Din Rumi, from *The Illuminated Rumi*, trans. Coleman Barks and illus. Michael Green (New York: Broadway Books, 1997), 77.

3. Ruth C. Duck, "Lead On, O Cloud of Yahweh," from *Ever-flowing Streams: Songs for Worship*, eds. Ruth C. Duck and Michael G. Bausch (New York: The Pilgrim Press, 1981), 77.

The First Gift of Waiting: Patience

1. Lao-tzu, *Tao Te Ching*, trans. Stephen Mitchell (New York: HarperCollins Publishers, 1988), 15.

2. Rachel Naomi Remen, M.D., *My Grandfather's Blessings: Stories of Strength, Refuge, and Belonging* (New York: Riverhead Books, 2000), 162-63.

3. *The New Testament and Psalms: An Inclusive Version*, eds. Victor Roland Gold et al. (New York: Oxford University Press, 1995), 294.

4. Pierre Teilhard de Chardin, from a letter to his cousin Marguerite Teilhard, July 4, 1915 in *The Making of a Mind: Letters from*

a Soldier-Priest 1914-1919, R. Hague, trans. (New York: Collins, 1965), 57.

5. Madeleine L'Engle, *The Irrational Season* (New York: The Seabury Press, 1977), 90.

6. Jack Kornfield, *A Path with Heart: A Guide through the Perils and Promises of Spiritual Life* (New York: Bantam Books, 1993), 81.

7. Donald P. McNeill, Douglas A. Morrison, and Henri J. M. Nouwen, *Compassion: A Reflection on the Christian Life* (Garden City, N.Y.: Doubleday & Company, Inc., 1983), 93.

8. Tzu, *Tao Te Ching*, 15.

The Second Gift of Waiting: Loss of Control

1. Rainer Maria Rilke, "Requiem for a Friend," from *The Selected Poetry of Rainer Maria Rilke*, ed. and trans. Stephen Mitchell (New York: Random House, 1982), 85.

2. *The Random House Dictionary of the English Language, Second Edition*, Unabridged ed. Flexner (New York: Random House, Inc., 1987), 1640.

3. Stephen V. Doughty, "Thoughts Towards and From the Second Surrender," *Weavings* 12, no. 2 (March/April 1997): 41. I am also indebted to Stephen Doughty for his vocabulary of being "hollowed" and "yielding."

4. Kornfield, *A Path with Heart*, 35.

5. Christina Baldwin, *Life's Companion: Journal Writing as a Spiritual Quest* (New York: Bantam Books, 1991), 99.

6. Mary Pipher, Ph.D., *The Middle of Everywhere: The World's Refugees Come to Our Town* (New York: Harcourt, Inc., 2002), 63.

7. Marilyn Chandler McEntyre, "What to Do in the Darkness," *Weavings* 19, no. 2 (March/April 2004): 27.

8. Baldwin, *Life's Companion*, 99.

The Third Gift of Waiting: Living in the Present

1. Thich Nhat Hanh, *Living Buddha, Living Christ* (New York: Riverhead Books, 1995), 14.

2. Lucy Grealy, *Autobiography of a Face* (New York: Houghton Mifflin Company, 1994), 116.

3. Etty Hillesum, *An Interrupted Life and Letters from Westerbork* (New York: Henry Holt and Company, 1996), 218.

4. Elizabeth A. Dreyer, *Earth Crammed with Heaven: A Spirituality of Everyday Life* (Mahwah, N.J.: Paulist Press, 1994), 140.

5. Eckhart Tolle, *The Power of Now: A Guide to Spiritual Enlightenment* (Novato, Calif.: New World Library, 1997), 71.

The Fourth Gift of Waiting: Compassion

1. Hafiz, "A Hunting Party," from *The Gift: Poems by Hafiz, The Great Sufi Master*, trans. Daniel Ladinsky (New York: Penguin/ Arkana, 1999), 26.

2. Remen, *My Grandfather's Blessings*, 350.

3. *The Sayings of the Desert Fathers*, trans. Benedicta Ward (Kalamazoo, Mich.: Cistercian Publications, 1975), 104.

4. Roberta Bondi offers an amazing discussion on what it means to receive well in her book *A Place to Pray: Reflections on the Lord's Prayer* (Nashville: Abingdon Press, 1998), 70-74.

5. Martha Beck, *The Joy Diet: 10 Daily Practices for a Happier Life* (New York: Crown Publishers, 2003), 182.

6. Rachel Naomi Remen, M.D., *Kitchen Table Wisdom: Stories That Heal* (New York: Riverhead Books, 1996), 244.

7. Marilyn S. Hair, M.Div., "Bridging the Challenges: The Effects of FOP on the Family," *Journal of Religion, Disability, and Health* 3, no. 3 (1999): 21.

8. Victor Parachin, "How Hope Can Help You Cope," *Exclusively Yours* (February 2003): 33.

9. *The Book of Common Prayer According to the Use of the Episcopal Church* (New York: Oxford University Press, 1979), 794.

10. Adapted from a Buddhist tonglen prayer taught by Rhea Emmer at her "Tending the Mystic Heart" retreat, The Center to Be, Milwaukee, Wisconsin, March 4, 2004.

The Fifth Gift of Waiting: Gratitude

1. *Meditations with Meister Eckhart*, trans. Matthew Fox (Santa Fe, N.Mex.: Bear & Company, 1983), 34.

2. Baldwin, *Life's Companion*, 343.

3. Fred Craddock, "Hearing God's Blessing," *The Christian Century* 107, no. 7 (January 24, 1990): 74.

4. Debbie Ford, *Spiritual Divorce: Divorce as a Catalyst for an Extraordinary Life* (New York: HarperSanFrancisco, 2001), 161-62.

5. Timothy Miller, Ph.D., *How to Want What You Have: Discovering the Magic and Grandeur of Ordinary Existence* (New York: Henry Holt and Company, 1995), 169.

6. Margaret Silf, *Close to the Heart: A Guide to Personal Prayer* (Chicago: Loyola Press, 1999), 59-60.

7. Idea from Kay Leigh Hagan, *Prayers to the Moon: Exercises in Self-Reflection* (New York: HarperSanFrancisco, 1991), 160.

8. Idea from Wayne Muller, *Sabbath: Restoring the Sacred Rhythm of Rest* (New York: Bantam Books, 1999), 202.

9. Lyn Klug, ed., *Soul Weavings: A Gathering of Women's Prayers* (Minneapolis: Augsburg Books, 1996), 40.

10. Baldwin, *Life's Companion*, 343.

The Sixth Gift of Waiting: Humility

1. Robert C. Morris, "Meek as Moses: Humility, Self-Esteem, and the Service of God," *Weavings* 15, no. 3 (May/June 2000): 37-38.

2. Information about Hillary Clinton and Henri Nouwen's invitation to the White House is from Wayne Muller, *Sabbath*, 174-75.

3. Jack Kornfield, *After the Ectasy, the Laundry: How the Heart Grows Wise on the Spiritual Path* (New York: Bantam Books, 2000), x.

4. Ibid., x.

5. *The Cloud of Unknowing*, trans. Clifton Wolters (Baltimore: Penguin Books, 1961), 71.

6. Joan Chittister, *The Rule of Benedict: Insights for the Ages* (New York: Crossroad, 1992), 73.

7. *An Inclusive Language Lectionary: Readings for Year A* (The Cooperative Publication Association, 1983), Lent 4, Lesson 1.

8. Keith Beasley-Topliffe, "Praying to Be Abandoned," *Weavings* 15, no. 3 (May/June 2000): 32.

9. Marianne Williamson, *A Return to Love: Reflections on the Principles of a Course in Miracles* (New York: HarperPerennial, 1993), 190-91.

The Seventh Gift of Waiting: Trust in God

1. Teresa of Avila, "Efficacy of Patience," from *The Collected Works of St. Teresa of Avila, Volume Three*, trans. Kieran Kavanaugh, O.C.D. and Otilio Rodriguez, O.C.D (Washington D.C.: Institute of Carmelite Studies, 1985), 386.

2. *The New Testament and Psalms: An Inclusive Version*, 489.

3. Denise Levertov, *A Door in the Hive* (New York: New Directions Publishing Corporation, 1984), 88.

4. Elizabeth A. Hamrick-Stowe, *Expecting: A Christian Exploration of Pregnancy and Childbirth* (Valley Forge, Penn.: Judson Press, 1979), 89.

5. Inspired by Anne Lamott, *Traveling Mercies: Some Thoughts on Faith* (New York: Pantheon Books, 1999), 131.

6. Thomas Merton, "Some Predispositions for Prayer" (a conference on prayer), cited in Jane Redmont, *When in Doubt, Sing: Prayer in Daily Life* (New York: HarperCollinsPublishers, 1999), 25.

7. Wayne Muller, *Learning to Pray: How We Find Heaven on Earth* (New York: Bantam Books, 2003), 74.

8. Bernard Thorogood, "Unsleeping Friend," from *Prayers Encircling the World: An International Anthology* (Louisville: Westminster John Knox Press, 1998), 131.

9. Roberta C. Bondi, *A Place to Pray*, 83.

10. Sequoyah prayer from Muller, *Learning to Pray*, 71.

Retreat: "A Spirituality of Waiting"

1. *The New Testament and Psalms: An Inclusive Version,* 522.

2. Ruth C. Duck, "Lead On, O Cloud of Yahweh" from *Ever-flowing Streams,* 77.

3. Debbie Perlman, "For Reassurance," *Flames to Heaven: New Psalms for Healing and Praise* (Wilmette, Ill.: Rad Publishers, 1998), 26.

Selected Bibliography

Baldwin, Christina. *Life's Companion: Journal Writing as a Spiritual Quest.* New York: Bantam Books, 1991.

Barks, Coleman, and Michael Green. *The Illuminated Rumi.* New York: Broadway Books, 1997.

Beasley-Topliffe, Keith. "Praying to Be Abandoned," *Weavings* 15, no. 3 (May/June 2000): 26-34.

Beck, Martha. *The Joy Diet: 10 Daily Practices for a Happier Life.* New York: Crown Publishers, 2003.

Bondi, Roberta. *A Place to Pray: Reflections on the Lord's Prayer.* Nashville, Tenn.: Abingdon, 1998.

Bonhoeffer, Dietrich. *Letters and Papers from Prison.* New York: The Macmillan Company, 1953.

The Book of Common Prayer. New York: Oxford University Press, 1979.

Chittister, Joan. *The Rule of Benedict: Insights for the Ages.* New York: Crossroad, 1992.

Craddock, Fred. "Hearing God's Blessing." *The Christian Century* 107, no. 7 (January 24, 1990): 74.

de Chardin, Pierre Teilhard, *The Making of a Mind: Letters from a Soldier-Priest 1914-1919*, R. Hague, trans. (New York: Collins, 1965), 57.

Doughty, Stephen V. "Thoughts Towards and From the Second Surrender." *Weavings* 12, no. 2 (March/April 1997): 38-45.

Dreyer, Elizabeth A. *Earth Crammed with Heaven: A Spirituality of Everyday Life.* Mahwah, N.J.: Paulist Press, 1994.

Duck, Ruth C. and Michael G. Bausch, eds. *Everflowing Streams: Songs for Worship*. New York: The Pilgrim Press, 1981.

Ford, Debbie. *Spiritual Divorce: Divorce as a Catalyst for an Extraordinary Life*. New York: HarperSanFrancisco, 2001.

Fox, Matthew, trans. *Meditations with Meister Eckhart*. Santa Fe, N.M.: Bear & Company, 1983.

Gold, Victor Roland, et al., eds. *The New Testament and Psalms: An Inclusive Version*. New York: Oxford University Press, 1995.

Grealy, Lucy. *Autobiography of a Face*. New York: Houghton Mifflin Company, 1994.

Guenther, Margaret. *My Soul in Silence Waits: Meditations on Psalm 62*. Boston: Cowley Publications, 2000.

Hagan, Kay Leigh. *Prayers to the Moon: Exercises in Self-Reflection*. New York: HarperSanFrancisco, 1991.

Hair, Marilyn S., M.Div. "Bridging the Challenges: The Effects of FOP on the Family." *Journal of Religion, Disability, and Health* 3, no. 3 (1999): 5-23.

Hair, Marilyn, and Sarah Steele. "Sarah Sets Out on Her Own." *FOP Connection* 17, no. 1 (February 2004): 10-12. This publication is the journal of the International Fibrodysplasia Ossificans Progressiva Association.

Hambrick-Stowe, Elizabeth A. *Expecting: A Christian Exploration of Pregnancy and Childbirth*. Valley Forge, Pa.: Judson Press, 1979.

Hanh, Thich Nhat. *Living Buddha, Living Christ*. New York: Riverhead Books, 1995.

Hillesum, Etty. *An Interrupted Life and Letters from Westerbork*. New York: Henry Holt and Company, 1996.

An Inclusive Language Lectionary: Readings for Year A. The Cooperative Publication Association, 1983.

Jones, Alan, John O'Neal, with Diana Landau. *Seasons of Grace: The Life-Giving Practice of Gratitude*. Hoboken, N.J.: John Wiley & Sons, Inc., 2003.

Kavanaugh, Kieran, O.C.D., and Otilio Rodriguez, O.C.D., trans. *The Collected Works of Teresa of Avila, Volume Three*. Washington, D.C.: Institute of Carmelite Studies, 1985.

Klug, Lyn, ed. *Soul Weavings: A Gathering of Women's Prayers*. Minneapolis,: Augsburg Books, 1996.

Kornfield, Jack. *After the Ecstasy, the Laundry: How the Heart Grows Wise on the Spiritual Path.* New York: Bantam Books, 2000.

_____. *A Path with Heart: A Guide through the Perils and Promises of Spiritual Life.* New York: Bantam Books, 1993.

Ladinsky, Daniel James, trans. *The Gift: Poems by Hafiz, the Great Sufi Master.* New York: Penguin/Arkana, 1999.

Lamott, Anne. *Traveling Mercies: Some Thoughts on Faith.* New York: Pantheon Books, 1999.

L'Engle, Madeleine. *The Irrational Season.* New York: The Seabury Press, 1977.

Levertov, Denise. *A Door in the Hive.* New York: New Directions Publishing Corporation, 1984.

McEntyre, Marilyn Chandler. "What to Do in the Darkness." *Weavings* 19, no. 2 (March/April 2004): 27.

McNeill, Donald P., Douglas A. Morris, and Henri J. M. Nouwen. *Compassion: A Reflection of the Christian Life.* Garden City, N.Y.: Doubleday & Company, Inc., 1983.

Miller, Timothy, Ph.D. *How to Want What You Have: Discovering the Magic and Grandeur of Everyday Existence.* New York: Henry Holt and Company, 1995.

Mitchell, Stephen., ed. and trans. *The Selected Poetry of Rainer Maria Rilke.* New York: Random House, 1982.

_____. trans. *Tao Te Ching: A New English Version.* New York: HarperCollins Publishers, 1988.

Mogabgab, John S., ed. *Weavings* 15, no. 3 (May/June, 2000): entire issue on "Humility."

Morris, Robert C. "Meek as Moses: Humility, Self-Esteem, and the Service of God," *Weavings* 15, no. 3 (May/June 2000): 36-44.

Muller, Wayne. *Learning to Pray: How We Find Heaven on Earth.* New York: Bantam Books, 2003.

_____. *Sabbath: Restoring the Sacred Rhythm of Rest.* New York: Bantam Books, 1999.

Nelson, Gertrud Mueller. *To Dance with God: Family Ritual and Community Celebration.* Mahwah, N.J.: Paulist Press, 1986.

Nouwen, Henri J. M. "A Spirituality of Waiting: Being Alert to God's Presence in Our Lives." *Weavings* 2, no. 1 (January/February 1987): 6-17.

Parachin, Victor. "How Hope Can Help You Cope." *Exclusively Yours* (February 2003): 33-35.

Patchett, Ann. *Truth & Beauty: A Friendship.* New York: HarperCollins-Publishers, 2004.

Perlman, Debbie. *Flames to Heaven: New Psalms for Healing and Praise.* Wilmette: Ill.: Rad Publishers, 1998.

Pipher, Mary, Ph.D. *Another Country: Navigating the Emotional Terrain of Our Elders.* Rockland, Mass.: Wheeler Publishing, Inc., 1999.

_____. *The Middle of Everywhere: The World's Refugees Come to Our Town.* New York: Harcourt, Inc., 2002.

Prayers Encircling the World: An International Anthology. Louisville: Westminster John Knox Press, 1998.

Prevallet, Elaine. "Borne in Courage and Love: Reflections on Letting Go." *Weavings* 12, no. 2 (March/April 1997): 6-15.

Redmont, Jane. *When In Doubt, Sing: Prayer in Daily Life.* New York: Harper-CollinsPublishers, 1999.

Remen, Rachel Naomi, M.D. *Kitchen Table Wisdom: Stories That Heal.* New York: Riverhead Books, 1996.

_____. *My Grandfather's Blessings: Stories of Strength.* New York: Riverhead Books, 2000.

Silf, Margaret. *Close to the Heart: A Guide to Personal Prayer.* Chicago: Loyola Press, 1999.

Steele, Richard. "Unremitting Compassion: Caring for a Special Needs Child Brings Suffering—and Growth." *Response* 22, no 3 (Summer 1999): 4-5. This publication is a newsletter of Seattle Pacific University.

Tolle, Eckhart. *The Power of Now: A Guide to Spiritual Enlightenment.* Novato, Calif.: New World Library, 1997.

Waite, Terry. *Taken on Trust.* New York: Quill/William Morrow, 1993.

Ward, Benedicta, trans. *The Sayings of the Desert Fathers.* Kalamazoo, Mich: Cistercian Publications, 1975.

Whitcomb, Holly W. *Feasting with God: Adventures in Table Spirituality.* Cleveland, Ohio: United Church Press, 1996.

_____. *Practicing Your Path: A Book of Retreats for an Intentional Life.* Minneapolis: Augsburg Books, 2002.

Williamson, Marianne. *A Return to Love: Reflections on the Principles of a Course in Miracles.* New York: HarperPerennial, 1993.

Wolters, Clifton, trans. *The Cloud of Unknowing.* Baltimore: Penguin Books, 1961.

Acknowledgments

Thank you . . .

Marcia Broucek, persevering and brilliant editor, for shaping this book into what it was meant to be;

Bonnie Andrews, friend and manuscript reader, for offering time and invaluable advice;

Chris Glaser, friend and colleague and author;

The Rev. Dr. Karl Kuhn, scholar and teacher;

Peg Koller, open-hearted friend and reference librarian;

Kind and generous reference librarians at the Elm Grove Public Library: Susan Freitag, Maxine Keene, Diane Meyer, Rita Miziorko, Sarah Muench, Karen Wood, and Director, Sheila O'Brien;

Nancy Massnick, Director of the Hartland Public Library;

Nancy Vollbrecht, inspirer and creative companion;

Kathleen Adams, confidante and friend;

Members of the Wisconsin Go-Hiking Club, who keep me fit and sane;

All of my retreatants and spiritual direction seekers, who teach me by sharing their paths to faith and wisdom;

My husband, John, and our children, David and Kate, who hold me safely in their love.

About the Author

Holly Wilson Whitcomb has been a pastor and clergy-woman in the United Church of Christ since her graduation from Yale Divinity School in 1978, and has served churches in Connecticut, Iowa, and Wisconsin. She is also a graduate of the two-year training program for spiritual directors at the Shalem Institute for Spiritual Formation in Bethesda, Maryland. As the Director of Kettlewood Retreats, Holly travels to churches, retreat houses, and conference centers to lead retreats and spirituality events around the country. She is also a spiritual director offering one-to-one spiritual direction. As a jewelry-maker and designer, she frequently incorporates "art as meditation" into her retreats and has donated a number of her pieces to charity auctions. In addition, Holly is an avid hike leader with a Wisconsin hiking club and loves the outdoors. She is the author of dozens of articles on spirituality and the author of three previous books, including *Feasting with God* and *Practicing Your Path*. She lives in a suburb of Milwaukee, Wisconsin. She and her husband, John, have two young-adult children, David and Kate.

You may contact Holly W. Whitcomb by calling the Kettlewood Retreats Office at (262) 784-5593 or by sending e-mail to hwhitcomb@wi.rr.com.

Other Resources from Augsburg

Soul Weavings by Lyn Klug
160 pages, 0-8066-2849-9

These rich, strong prayers reflect the needs and experiences of women of all ages. They are gathered from historic and contemporary women of faith from around the world.

Practicing Your Path by Holly W. Whitcomb
128 pages, 0-8066-9018-6

An invitation to rebalance your life and regain perspective. Offers seven one-day retreats on the components of classical Christian spirituality. Each chapter includes a structure for a one-day private retreat with flexible options for groups.

How to Keep a Spiritual Journal by Ron Klug
144 pages, 0-8066-4357-9

This revised edition of a thorough guide offers steps for anyone interested in keeping a spiritual journal, from recommendations for notebooks to ways to work through common frustrations and writer's block.

Sabbath Sense by Donna E. Schaper
128 pages, 0-8066-9017-8

Sabbath as a day of rest has been lost in our to-do lists and organizers, but the sense of Sabbath, as spiritual leisure, is very much needed in our time-starved world. *Sabbath Sense* offers a refreshing perspective on making the spiritual choice to take back our time, one moment at a time.

Available wherever books are sold.

LaVergne, TN USA
02 November 2009
162818LV00008B/63/P